The Basics of Western Riding

by Charlene Strickland

Foreword by Martha Josey

Illustrated by Elayne Sears

STOREY

Storey Books

The mission of Storey Communications is to serve our customers
by publishing practical information that encourages personal independence
in harmony with the environment.

Edited by Elizabeth Anne McHale
Cover design by Meredith Maker
Cover photograph © Gemma Giannini. Back cover photos © (top to bottom) Reneé Stockdale, Gemma Giannini, Charlene
    Strickland, and Jeff Vanuga.
Text design and production by Mark Tomasi, Susan Bernier and Eileen Clawson
Photographs by the author, unless otherwise noted. Photographs on pages 1 and 91 by Curtis Martin. Photographs on
    pages 28, 43, and 58 (top) by Cynthia McFarland. Photograph on page 74 by Reneé Stockdale.
Indexed by Susan Olason, Indexes & Knowledge Maps

The information in this book is true and complete to the best of our knowledge. All recommendations are made
without guarantee on the part of the author or Storey Books. The author and publisher disclaim any liability in
connection with the use of this information. For additional information, please contact Storey Books, Schoolhouse
Road, Pownal, Vermont 05261.

Storey Books are available for special premium and promotional uses and for customized editions. For further information, please call Storey's Custom Publishing Department at 1-800-793-9396.

Printed in Canada by Transcontinental Printing
10 9 8 7 6 5 4 3 2

Library of Congress Cataloging-in-Publication Data

Strickland, Charlene.
    The basics of western riding / by Charlene Strickland ;
    illustrated by Elayne Sears; foreword by Martha Josey.
        p.   cm.
    Includes bibliographical references and index.
     ISBN 1-58017-030-7 (pbk. : alk. paper)
     1. Western riding.   I. Title.
SF309.3.S823 1998
798.2'3—dc21   97-46770

Contents

Acknowledgments

In barns, beside pickup trucks, or leaning against the top rail of the corral — Western riders and trainers can't stop talking horses. I've listened and learned from these experts over the years, and here's thanks to these Westerners (and a few Easterners, too!) for sharing their expertise:

Horse Show Judges

Don Burt
Jim Baker
Peggy Jo Koll
Brian Ellsworth

Pete Wood
Walter de la Brosse
Whizzer Baker

Trainers

Jim Porcher — Arabians and national show horses
Alpha Russell — Appaloosas, Western equitation
Casey Hinton — Quarter horses
Mack Linn — Stock seat equitation
Mike Baker — Reining
Terry Berg — Western pleasure
Nancy Cahill — Stock seat equitation
Carolyn Bader — Trail horse class
Dave Moore — Western riding class
Tom Sorensen — Reining
Terry McCutcheon — Stock seat equitation, roping
Maggi McHugh — Trail horse, stock seat equitation
Harold Farren — Horse training, reining
Larry Gimple — Western pleasure
Joe King — Western pleasure, reining
Jack Baker — Horse training, reining
Gary Ferguson — Reining, stock seat equitation
Gill Swarbrick — Stock seat equitation
Lonny Shirk — Western pleasure
Andy Moorman — Stock seat equitation
Chuck Briggs — Stock seat equitation
Andrea Simons — Showmanship
Jon Higginson — Western riding class
Danny Gerardi — Reining
Sandy Collier — Reined cow horse
Todd Sommers — Western pleasure, reining
Guy Stoops — Western pleasure
Tim McQuay — Reining
Jim McCarty — Reining
Randy Paul — Reining

Bob and Dolly Wallace — Reining, working cow horse
Carl McCuistion — Working cow horse
Tom Lyons — Cutting
Barbara Schulte — Cutting
Rob Little — Cutting
Scott Sheldon — Cutting
Tony Boit — Reining
Don West — Trail riding
Victor Kerr — Horse training, showing
Traci Vanek — Stock seat equitation
Mark Taylor — Western pleasure
Dave Rhodes — Stock seat equitation
Linda Tellington-Jones — Horse training
John Richard Young — Horse training, stock seat equitation
Monty Roberts — Horse training
John Lyons — Horse training
Pat Parelli — Horse training, stock seat equitation
Talmadge Green — Barrel racing
Ross Carnahan — Pole bending
Wes Hough — Roping

Riders and Contestants

Becky Hart — Endurance riding
Amy Nichols and Javier Soto — Endurance riding
Heidi Caldwell — Endurance riding
Audrey Taylor — Competitive trail riding
Lisa Skyhorse — Ride and tie
Eugenie (Oogie) McGuire — Mules
Jill Pennau — Horse showing
Lela Kay French — Horse showing

Wendy Bagley — Reining
Angelo Berrettini — Reining
Kim Verville — Cutting
Cheryl Lucero — Barrel racing
John and Stephanie Essman — Barrel racing
Alegra Padilla — Timed events
Elaina Chavez — Timed events
Chad Crider — Pole bending
Elisha Aker — Timed events
Shannon Gribling — Timed events
Andy Luna — Roping
Patty, Tona, Jana, Koell, and Leona Wright — Roping, timed events
Dan, Jeanette, Chezie, Kelsey, Megan, and Pecos Davis — Roping, timed events
Anita Roy — Team penning
Peggy Lewis — Team penning
Bob Hyatt — Team penning
Deann Warrick — Rodeo queen

Associations and Businesses

Rick Sykes — National Barrel Horse Association
Mike McMillian — International Halter-Pleasure Quarter Horse Association
Raeana Wadhams — Miss Rodeo America
Randy Bernhardt — National FFA Foundation
Cole Smith — Smith Brothers Ropes
Jim Bullock, DVM
Bruce Blake — Lexington Safety Products
Carl Swenson — Reed Hill, Inc.

Foreword

Western riding has been a major part of my life and career, and so I am extremely honored to write the Foreword for this book.

Western riding is many things to many different people. To me, it is an art, a gift, and a way of life. I have been fortunate, through more than thirty years of competing and instructing, to have seen Western riding as an avenue to build confidence, self-esteem, and skill in people of all ages.

From the Western pleasure arena, to the rodeo grounds, and to the ranches of the world, Western riding is used to bring out the best our equine partners have to offer. Although the various events differ, the fundamental skills remain the same and are developed through years of practice.

I love to be known as a barrel racer, but what I strive to be is a cowgirl. I want to understand how horses work and why. I have ridden reining and cutting horses, and, believe it or not, even a bull or two in my time. Whether it is judging horses, barrel racing, or working a pleasure class, good ole' horse sense can be used to correlate what you know with something you may just be learning about: This is what makes Western riding such a challenge. It is a living art, worthy of constant study.

Children everywhere have played cowboys and Indians, riding across the vast prairies of their neighborhoods and backyards on imaginary horses. Some of them are fortunate enough to receive the incredible gift of a horse to ride. A few of them grow up to participate in the equine industry, fulfilling dreams that usually come true only in the movies. There are many different opportunities that can arise from Western riding. There is a great demand for riding instructors, clinicians, horse sales, and show management. Veterinarians and breeding specialists are also in high demand because of advances in technology.

Who would have ever guessed that my husband R. E. and I would travel throughout the country giving barrel racing, calf roping, and horsemanship clinics. Not only have we had this great opportunity, but I have also competed in the Olympics, the NFR, the AQHA World Show and Congress, as well as the National Barrel Horse Association World Championships. These spectacular opportunities were dreams come true for my husband and me. We now have some of the best clinics in the world, and our Josey World Champion Jr. Barrel Race is the premiere barrel race for young people in the world. With a lot of hard work and determination, you too can experience the wonderful things I have been so fortunate to be involved in.

As a pastime, Western riding is used by many to escape life's daily pressures. How fortunate we are to be able to push ourselves to the limit, improving our horsemanship, physical fitness, and mental attitude while doing what we love — riding and being around horses. It is truly heartwarming for me to see the look in my students' eyes when they feel a sense of accomplishment after a clinic. They work diligently to achieve the fulfillment that riding can provide. Western riding teaches discipline, self-control, patience, and sportsmanship. These are invaluable lessons.

As a way of life, Western riding and the cowboy way provide me with many of the unwritten codes I live by. Dedication, hard work, equality, and loyalty are all positive by-products of Western riding. I live a busy life, filled with friends and family whom I could not live without. The good times shared with these people at the many different events we attend are very special to me. Through Western riding, you too will build a strong bond with the people in your life.

I feel confident you will enjoy this book, and may you be blessed, as I have been, with the art, the gift, and way of life of Western riding!

— Martha Josey

Martha Josey took the 1997 World Championship at the National Barrel Horse Association finals. She has won several National Barrel Horse Association World Championships and has also participated in the Olympics, the AQHA World Show, and the American Quarter Horse Congress. Martha and her husband R. E. run Josey Enterprises, the leader in barrel racing, roping, and horsemanship clinics; they have their own line of barrel racing and calf-roping equipment. Visit their web site at www.barrelracers.com or contact Josey Enterprises, Inc., at JoseyRanch@barrelracers.com.

The Tradition of Western Riding

Partners — horse and rider — can share the freedom and adventure of the Old West. Whether it's a Pinto, golden Palomino, or Appaloosa, a sturdy horse can transport the equestrian into a uniquely American sport.

Seated in a Western saddle, you can mosey along a desert path, lope across a mountain meadow, or gallop your horse pell-mell down a hill in pursuit of a wily steer. Choose your level of excitement; when you grab the horn and swing up into the saddle, you relive the nostalgia of riding the range.

Like the West itself, riding perpetuates the traditions of a romantic past, yet it is a contemporary recreation. The horse keeps the sport vibrant and real, not artificial or pretentious.

You can pursue many types of Western riding. Even today, you can roam the same country that the frontiersmen and pioneers traveled. You can escape into the plain, down-in-the-dirt action that is as rustic as the lives of Jesse James and Billy the Kid were. If you just want to ponder the solitary pleasures of the trail, you can listen to the creak of saddle leather and the steps of your horse. If competition is in your blood, you can choose your arena — from the trail to horse shows to cattle-roping events. Whatever you choose, all trace their origins to the legendary American cowboy.

The Legend of the Cowboy

Around the world, equestrians admire the cowboy as a heroic figure. He lived a rigorous lifestyle. His life was clear-cut, clean, pastoral, close to the rhythms of nature. When you think of a cowboy, you envision a set of values: independence, simplicity, courage, toughness, and grace.

The cowhand practiced these values on horseback. With his equine partner, he deftly performed physical tasks with skill. He proved himself

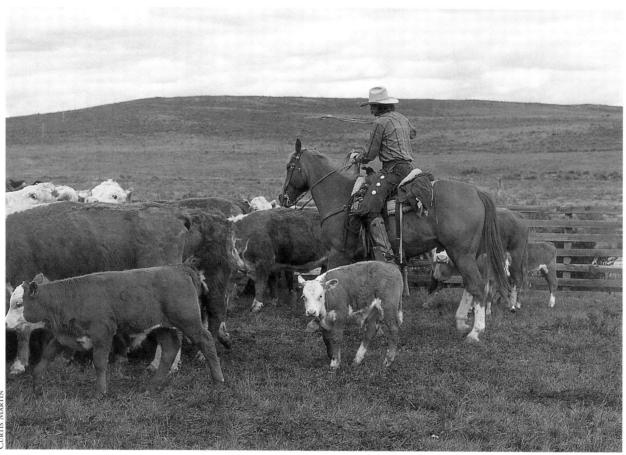

With the help of his horse, the cowboy continually tested his competence in handling livestock.

genuinely competent at horsemanship and handling livestock — driving cattle, cutting calves, and roping steers.

That mystique continues to stir the imagination. The figure of the lean, weathered cowboy perpetuates the thrills of the American frontier. When you sit on a stock horse, you can re-enact those long, dusty days of cattle work, or display equestrian elegance in the precision of exact movements. You can share a rapture, the sense of freely riding a horse through a landscape.

Western riding gives you an escape. On a typical weekday, you wrestle with machines of all types — a toaster, a car, a microwave, a computer, a cash register. Machines force you to conform to their rules.

Dealing with a horse puts you in charge. Horses aren't robotic, and you would never treat them with a blasé attitude. Horses are delightful, unpredictable creatures that are capable of more

emotional connection than you'd expect from a beast of burden.

Western riding also exposes you to risk. The cowboy accepted risk as part of his daily life, and his courage survives today in rodeo contestants. Rodeo cowboys set the style for today's Western ethic. In rodeo, athletes compete without the protective devices so prevalent in other sports. Rodeo seems to fly in the face of a society obsessed with safety precautions and the threat of litigation.

When you ride Western, you're making a statement. You choose an alternative to a lifestyle of peace and boredom. Risk appeals to you. You seek the vigor of days past and the companionship of the cowboy's most important buddy, the horse.

Anyone can emulate the cowboy's back-to-basics approach to horsemanship. Few, however, can claim to be cowboys, earning a living by working on a ranch. But, for the price of admission,

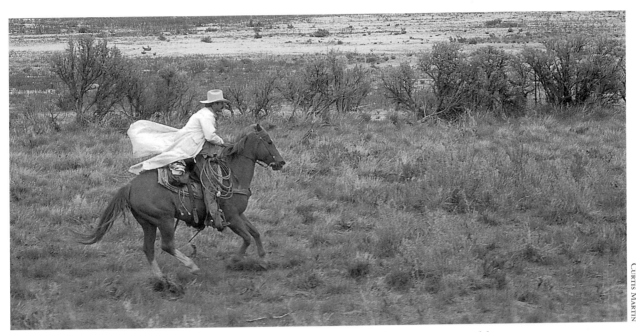

Western riding nurtures a proud free spirit and relies on the trust between man and horse.

you can associate with authentic cowhands on professional dude ranches. There you can rub elbows with real cowboys and cowgirls who make their living on ranches. It's a unique opportunity to learn the traditions of Western horsemanship from genuine horsemen. On dude ranches, cowboys and cowgirls are the mentors who communicate the traditions of Western horsemanship.

The Tradition

Western riding developed from the same foundation as other riding disciplines. European masters studied the classical principles of equitation in the sixteenth century, and their contemporaries conquered the Americas.

Spanish conquerors founded Western horsemanship in their seat and saddlery, which also influenced the military riding traditions of the world's cavalry forces. European horsemen studied horsemanship so they could wage war. Spain, France, and Italy developed similar schools of riding, all using saddles with a high pommel and cantle and long stirrups. This Moorish design held the warrior in place during long marches and the dangers of battle.

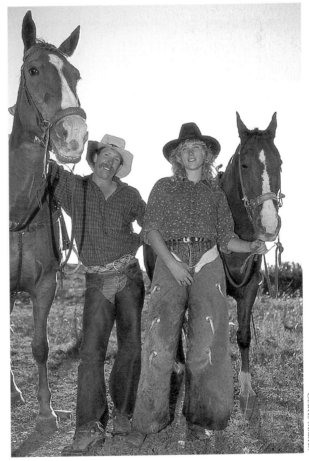

On dude ranches, cowboys and cowgirls communicate the traditions of Western horsemanship.

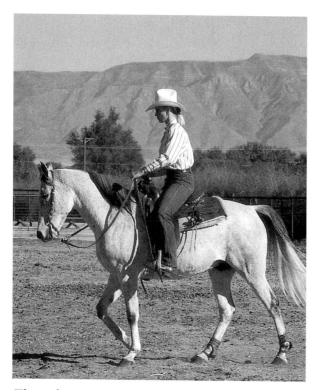

The goal in Western riding is graceful, unified movement at any speed.

The Spanish riding style used a deep, balanced seat, similar to that practiced today at Vienna's Spanish Riding School. Riders relied on the powerful curb bit to keep the horse collected, and they used spurs with large rowels to cue the horse. (A rowel is a small wheel with points, attached to the shank of a spur.)

As Spain expanded its military frontiers in North America, Spaniards spread their culture throughout the American West. The vaqueros followed the traditions of the Old World, using Spanish methods of handling livestock on the vast ranches.

The vaquero evolved into the cowboy, who remained a man of the horse. Other riders also adapted European ways, riding styles, and saddlery to their needs. On the vast spaces of the frontier, horsemanship was a critical skill. The horse was necessary to the Westerner's work of expanding the frontier and establishing cattle ranches.

The horse extended man's mobility and gave individual freedom. As Easterners moved West, through the Great Plains toward the Great American Desert, they relied on equine power to traverse geographical barriers. Horses were used in exploration, hunting, cattle drives, war, and all types of commerce. Horsemen and their horses built the West.

Horsemanship Today

Western riding has progressed a long way since early cattle drives. Today the masters blend the ways of the West with classic equitation and aim for a smooth horse that performs without resistance.

The archetypal cowboy was supremely comfortable on a horse. Like all expert horsemen, he demonstrated an elite skill. Today's horseman maintains that proud, free spirit and nurtures the trust between himself and his horse.

The wise horseman conserves his mount's energy. He moves in a low-key manner, quietly telling his horse what to do. He knows when to take command, such as telling his horse to gallop to head off a determined steer. He also senses when to let the horse choose its moves, such as when walking slowly on a treacherous mountain trail.

JEFF VANUGA

Horse and rider concentrate on a single goal — full speed ahead!

Western Riding Activities

Sport	Description	Appeal
Trail Riding	Riding horse along a path Can be informal, or organized for a group	Slow-paced Pleasant
Distance Riding	Riding a marked trail, judged by (1) horse's condition at finish, (2) time, and (3) horsemanship	Competitive situation Allows you to prove your horsemanship in preparing the horse and conquering the course
Show Riding	Prepares horse and rider to compete in association's events	Show off horse and horsemanship Dress up Win prizes
Halter Classes	Show horse of any age in breed shows	Exhibit your animal Win prizes
Reining	Ride a pattern at speed	Follow a precise pattern Win prizes
Cutting	Sort through a herd of cattle, separate a cow, and prevent it from rejoining the herd	Thrill of riding a horse with cow sense Win prizes
Roping	Run after a calf or steer, and rope it	Enjoy the teamwork as your horse positions you so you can rope the cow easily Win prizes
Team Penning	You and 2 other riders separate 3 steers from a herd and chase them into a pen	Enjoy the teamwork of your horse and your fellow riders

RENEÉ STOCKDALE

In team roping, timing is crucial. Aim for consistency before you develop speed.

Team penning requires handy horses, alert riders, team spirit, and luck.

Horse and rider move in harmony, as closely attuned as a dressage pair. Yet unlike the dressage rider who controls his horse with constant contact with reins, the Western rider can make his horse do his bidding on a loose rein.

Horsewoman Terry Berg has compared the Western horse to his English counterpart. "People think because you use a bigger bit, you're cruel. But all you have to do is ride a horse that gives lightly when all you've done is barely pick up the reins. You may not even take the slack out of the reins. Your hand comes up slightly, and the horse responds. There's nothing like it — it's fabulous."

With the effective touch of the rein, the horse obeys every command. He immediately adjusts speed or direction or impulsion at the rider's slightest cue.

The movement is graceful, unified, and coordinated at any speed. The rider doesn't display emotion as he communicates his wishes. The horse responds to gentle handling, accelerating with quiet excitement and returning to a calm state.

Riding is a skill, and horsemanship is a special relationship between two partners. The horse teaches the rider, and the rider teaches the horse. When they become attuned, they reach the ultimate — the horse becomes an extension of the horseman.

In past centuries and cultures, this talent was passed down through generations. A horseman was born into it, and he naturally absorbed knowledge from mentors both human and equine. Chances are, you didn't grow up riding horses every day, sitting in front of Dad's saddle or piloting your own pony. Even if you were not "born in the saddle," you can consciously study to gain physical skill and the horseman's mental attitude. Today you can gain this expertise, whether or not you live in the West.

This handbook introduces you to all facets of Western riding. It communicates the excitement of casual trail rides, the fundamentals of horse handling, and the challenges of becoming a Western rider. The information in this book assumes you're an amateur, seeking a leisure activity as well as the sport's physical and spiritual pleasures.

Western disciplines vary, and most riders specialize. Few horses and riders sucessfully cross over into different areas, although you and your horse may enjoy the variety of other activities.

This book will guide you from preparation to performance of each Western riding discipline.

You'll learn the basics as well as how to refine your horsemanship skills.

Authorities across the United States, from Florida to California, have contributed their advice and offered strategies for success. Champions in every discipline, judges, and proficient riders have shared their philosophies and methods. You'll find that occasionally these experts' opinions conflict, but this is the equestrian tradition — every horseman has an opinion about the "right way."

If you're new to the sport, expect months of practicing before you really know how to ride a horse and years more before you're worthy of the term *horseman*.

But first, begin by picking your partner — the Western horse.

The Western Horse

The horse that carries you across pastures, around the show ring, or up mountainous trails reflects the characteristics of his ancestors — the horses that built the West. Sure, you can cinch up a Western saddle on a Thoroughbred, or even a European Warmblood, but these horses are not Western horses.

The Western, or stock, horse was bred to handle livestock. Horses and cattle were essential to life. Ranchers raised cattle as a source of food and sign of prosperity, and they needed stock horses to work the cattle.

The horses of the West had to outrun cattle and let the cowboy drive, rope, or drag a cow. Spanish horses, bred for the ranches and bullrings of Iberia, also worked cattle in the West. The first cowboys, the vaqueros, sought mounts with the speed and strength to handle the wild range cattle they chased across the plains.

Horses of the West also served as beasts of burden. They carried riders long distances, pulled wagons and coaches, and packed supplies and goods across the terrain. The Western horse symbolized power.

The horse made America, and the geography of the West influenced the type of horse that thrived. The Spanish conquerors of the sixteenth century brought the Barb horse to the New World. Originally from the Barbary region of North Africa, the Barb and Arabian breeds accompanied the Moors to conquer Spain. Iberian horsemen developed the Spanish Barb, horses that helped the nation conquer others around the world. These graceful horses displayed spirit and a proud carriage. The Barb influenced breeds across Europe, and even horses of the English colonists originated from Spanish blood.

The Spanish horse was an important commodity in North America. This animal was short-backed, with shorter legs than the modern Western horse. He was sure-footed and could carry his rider through the stress of battle. A durable animal, he could withstand extreme conditions. Spanish horses showed all colors, including spotted horses, buckskins, and Palominos.

Introduced to the American West around 1600, Spanish horses flourished. Their descendants were smaller, short-legged, chunky animals, fitted to enduring hard work. Ranchers and some Native Americans practiced selective breeding, but many horses ran wild. Natural selection altered these wild animals, and those that survived were adapted to tough conditions.

The horse's endurance and strong build made it reliable on long rides. The horse worked cattle on trail drives, traveling 10 to 15 miles per day. When pressed, a rider could push his horse to cover 40, 80, or as much as 100 miles a day.

A rider afoot was in great danger, so the horse was a crucial partner and the cowboy's most valued tool. On a tough mount, the cowboy was safe from wild longhorns and could control livestock.

Riders chose certain horses to handle stock. The cow horse had to have the spirit to "chouse" (round up) cattle and the speed to overtake a galloping cow. Once the horse caught up to a cow, steer, or bull, he had to display the courage to control the animal. Cowboys quickly learned that horses of Spanish heritage demonstrated more "cow sense" than animals of English descent.

Westerners favored a horse built for short bursts of speed. Its close-coupled body, heavy shoulders, powerful loin and hindquarters, and dropped-off croup gave it the conformation to dig into the ground at the takeoff. Short cannon bones and muscled forearms and stifles supported the horse's weight and made the horse look stout, and good withers held a stock saddle in place.

The stock horse weighed from 1,000 to 1,100 pounds. He was able to run, stop, and turn quickly. With his small size and short legs, he was surefooted on uneven terrain and had good action to move over rocks. He carried his short neck low, which allowed him to watch his footing and increase his efficient movement by reducing wind resistance.

Bred to work, the Western horse was tough, physically and mentally. He could go long distances, and he withstood strenuous, demanding work for 8 to 12 hours a day.

The Spanish Barb displays surefootedness and proud carriage. The horse's endurance and strong build make him reliable on long rides.

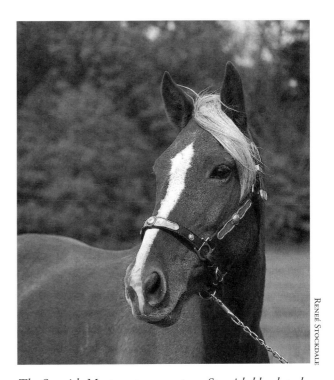

The Spanish Mustang preserves pure Spanish blood and is energetic and alert.

The Western Horse Today

Western horses inherited the stamina and agility of their Spanish progenitors. Spanish blood was crossed with horses from the East, adding the influence of the English Thoroughbred. From the horses of the nineteenth century, horsemen developed specific breeds.

Among the breeds, contemporary horses for Western riding are of three basic types: the reliable trail horse, the agile ranch horse, and the pretty show horse. Each breed may include animals of all types.

The Quarter Horse type dominates. Blending the hardy Spanish cow horse with the fast, graceful Thoroughbred, the early Quarter Horse displayed heavy muscle on the forearm, shoulder, loin, hip, and gaskin. He had a small head, broad chest, deep body, and short coupling.

The Quarter Horse earned a reputation as a horse built for speed that could run and work. Some Quarter Horses worked all week and raced on the weekend. They had the stamina to travel long days and were "good keepers." The breed's calm disposition and responsive attitude helped make this horse the world's most popular breed. Its versatility has influenced Western sports, and "America's Horse" continues to win major titles in racing, rodeo contests, cutting, reining, Western pleasure, and cattle events.

Except for the Spanish Barb and Mustang, horses of other breeds strongly resemble Quarter Horses. The color breeds incorporated Quarter Horse sires and dams, and most still register animals of Quarter Horse breeding.

Choosing Your First Horse

Acquiring a new horse can mean the realization of a lifelong dream. But as you search for the perfect match, keep in mind what you expect of your horse in its personality, performance, and appearance.

First and foremost, the type of horse you choose depends on the type of riding you plan to do. If you're just starting out, you want to pick the right partner for your riding career. Take the time to define your goals and shop wisely.

Try to rate a candidate objectively, without falling in love with a horse that might not fit your needs. If you're focusing on a certain riding discipline, pick a horse that matches that style. Don't choose one that's unfit for the type of riding you plan to do and then try to make him succeed.

In fact, Terry Berg advises to "go with what the horse is built to do. Just because you want him to be a Western Pleasure horse doesn't mean that's what he should do. A horse that isn't a natural mover for pleasure may be a good reining or roping horse."

Don't be afraid to enlist help to find your equine partner, ideally a mentor who can advise you. On your own, you can make a lot of mistakes. An authority can help steer you in the right direction and avoid frustrations. For example, you may envision buying a mare and raising a champion foal, but this challenges even the professionals. Don't even consider a stallion, which is a horse only for the expert horseman. A gelding is the most realistic choice for a first horse.

Be sure you find a qualified expert to advise you. A 4-H horse leader or college horsemanship instructor are ideal choices. You can also hire a professional to help you find and start with a new horse (be sure to check the horseman's credentials thoroughly). Hiring a trainer is like contracting for any other service. You make a list of local candidates who might meet your needs and then inquire about their qualifications. Talk to riders you know, breed and show officials, tack shops, feed stores, breeders, or even other trainers. No doubt you'll hear a range of opinions and individual viewpoints.

When you're ready to meet the trainer, introduce yourself and explain your goals. You're hiring her to perform a service, so you conduct an interview. Find out if this person wants you as a prospective customer and if your personalities mesh.

If you are new to horseback riding, you would benefit from taking riding lessons from an instructor. This professional can also help you find your

An expert horseman can help you choose the right horse.

own horse. You would learn the basics and gain confidence by riding school (lesson) horses, which have the temperament to tolerate beginners. You could spend several months or even a year developing horsemanship skills before you buy your own horse.

When you try out a horse, let the horse tell you about himself. Your friendship begins with these first impressions, so allow the animal to express his attributes through his body language. Observe how he reacts to all handling, on the ground and under saddle, and make a list of positive and negative points.

The horse's personality is key. To move in accord, the two of you must avoid personality clashes. Most people look for a tranquil companion, one that meets the description of "gentle." If you're an aggressive rider, you might prefer an amenable yet courageous partner. However, if you're more timid

and indecisive, you might enjoy a bolder animal that takes more initiative.

Investigate the horse's background as much as possible while he's in a familiar environment. Get used to handling and riding him while his owner or trainer is present. Under saddle, test the candidate on gymnastic movements to see how athletic he is, and simulate as many situations as you can while you test the horse.

Your mentor can help you rate the horse's previous schooling, disposition, and ability to excel in the type of riding you plan. You can ask about the horse's history of training and performance. Talk to a previous trainer if you can. You want to find out how the horse succeeded in his previous work. If the seller advertised the horse as a reining prospect, you may discover the horse competed in Western Pleasure. Why is he no longer showing as a pleasure horse?

Breed Comparisons

Breed	Physical Characteristics	Colors	Attributes	Association
Quarter Horse	Powerful loins and croup Sloping croup Stocky legs 15 hands 900–1,200 lbs.	Bay, brown, black, gray, palomino, dun [AQHA limits the extent of white markings. If horse has too much white for AQHA registration, he's a "cropout" and can be registered with APHA.]	Speed Calm disposition Agility Sure-footedness Rugged constitution	American Quarter Horse Association
Spanish Barb	Clean, well-defined head Deep, strong neck, chest, and body Average to short back Rounded croup and hip Proud carriage 14.2 hands 850–1,000 lbs.	All colors except gray and white	Stamina Agility Intelligence	Spanish Barb Breeders Association
Spanish Mustang	Sturdy, wiry, smooth body with long, smooth muscling Deep heart girth Short back Strong legs and feet Convex facial profile Arched neck Full mane and tail 13.2–15 hands 750–1,000 lbs.	Bay, chestnut, black, Appaloosa, dun, grulla, pinto, Medicine Hat, War Bonnet	Descendant of the Spanish horse, preserves pure Spanish blood Toughness, energy, endurance Naturally gaited Alert, even disposition	Spanish Mustang Registry

Appaloosa

Paint

Breed	Color/Coat Pattern	Bloodlines	Association
Appaloosa	Blanket, spots, blanket with spots, roan, roan blanket, roan blanket with spots Mottled skin White sclera Vertical stripes on hooves	One parent registered with ApHC Other parent may be AQHA, Thoroughbred, Arabian	Appaloosa Horse Club (ApHC)
Paint	Overo Tobiano Tovero No Appaloosa coat patterns	Both parents registered with APHA (or the former American Paint Quarter Horse Association or American Paint Stock Horse Association), AQHA, or Thoroughbred	American Paint Horse Association (APHA)
Pinto	Overo Tobiano Coat pattern meets specific color requirements White and colored markings are ideally 50–50 proportions No Appaloosa coat patterns	Parents registered with PtHA or approved outcross (AQHA, APHA, Thoroughbred, Standardbred)	Pinto Horse Association (PtHA)
Palomino	Golden coat with mane and tail a minimum of 85% white hairs No dun factor markings or body spots	Parents registered with PHBA or one PHBA parent and other AQHA, Thoroughbred, Morgan, Arabian, Part-Arabian	Palomino Horse Breeders Association (PHBA)
Buckskin	Buckskin, dun, red dun, grulla, brindle dun Dun factor markings: dorsal stripe, leg barring/mottling, shoulder stripe, rib barring, neck stripe/patches, face mask/cobwebbing, ear frames/barring, mane/tail frosting	Any stock horse meeting color requirements	American Buckskin Horse Association (ABHA) International Buckskin Horse Association (IBHA)

Pinto

Palomino

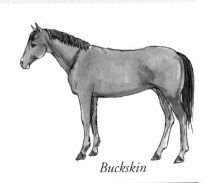

Buckskin

You won't be able to observe every behavior before you buy, so interview the seller. For example, how does the horse react to the farrier and the veterinarian? Will he accept all types of grooming, including bathing and clipping?

Also investigate the horse's diet. You'll want to continue the same type and amount of feed when you bring the horse to your barn. Does he receive any special supplements or medications? Does he have any unusual eating or drinking habits?

Examine the tack used on the horse. To ease the transition, plan to use similar, if not identical, equipment when you take the horse home. You might be able to purchase or borrow his familiar tack. If not, test your saddle and bridle on the horse to verify that they fit correctly.

With a registered horse, examine the registration papers. Read the description of color and markings and confirm that it matches the animal.

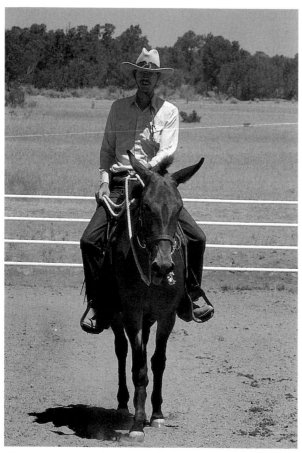

You may prefer riding a tough, durable mule. Mules are intelligent, curious, and sure-footed.

Pony or Mule?

You don't have to choose the conventional horse. You may prefer riding a horse sized to you, or a tough, durable mule: a horse mule (a gelded male) or a molly mule (mare).

The mule reflects its horse parent, so you have the choice of Quarter Horse, Paint, or Appaloosa mules. Distance riders often prefer a mule with a purebred or part-Arabian dam.

Mule riders consider themselves superior to those mounted on mere horses. A mule is the

Mule Characteristics	
Mule Fact	**Mule Fable**
Long ears Smaller, narrower feet Low withers Shorter hip and smaller, peaked hindquarters Longer back	Ugly
Intelligent and curious Level-headed Stays sound, has good sense of self-preservation Requires consistent, patient training and handling Needs time to adapt to change Develops close equine friendships Has a sense of humor	Stubborn Balky Nasty temperament
Great endurance Heat tolerance Long-lived	
Agile Sure-footed Steady mover Slow speed	Short-strided Rough gaits
Holds grudges Won't tolerate injustice Can aim kicks	Cunning and mean Always kicks
Resistant to water founder	Will never founder

offspring of a jack sire (male donkey) and a mare dam, and differs from a horse in several ways.

Many young riders start out with horses, but a pony may be more fun. Western ponies are scaled-down horses, which meet the same requirements as a riding horse. Despite his short stature, a pony can perform as well as a horse. He can turn fast and run hard. Some critics dislike the pony's gait, which may appear short-strided if compared to a horse. The Quarter Pony has Quarter Horse characteristics, and the Pony of the Americas looks similar to an Appaloosa.

An Objective Eye Before You Buy

You evaluate a performance horse by matching his potential with the sport you choose. Set aside your feelings about a particular horse, and take a close, objective look at him.

You want to see the horse in his natural, unprepared state. For this, you might stop by the barn without an appointment, or an hour ahead of a scheduled time. Yes, this might be impolite, but you want to see the horse before the seller prepares him for your visit. Lameness may be undetectable after the owner exercised the horse, but soreness can show up when you take the horse from his stall or corral.

Either you or your mentor can perform this observation. If you feel confident about doing this by yourself, use the checklist on pages 18–19 to study the horse. You should be able to recognize the basic signs of a healthy animal, as you're looking for deviations from the normal.

Don't worry about what the seller thinks, or let her intimidate you. You should have the right to investigate the horse carefully before deciding to purchase. You'll also learn more about the horse when you examine him thoroughly.

JUNE CAMPBELL

Although this mule wears an English bit and bridle, mules can also be used in Western riding. Look for your companion to express personality through body language.

JUNE CAMPBELL

Test any animal's manners before buying. If you're new to riding, you will need a horse or mule with a calm, sensible temperament.

Observe the Horse in His Stall

First look at the surroundings. Is the floor marked from the horse weaving or stallwalking? Does the door show signs of cribbing? And when you query the owner, does the person quickly make excuses about this horse not being in his usual stall?

Don't expect every seller to lie, but suspect anything that you hear. You're planning to make a major investment in money, time, and emotion, and you want to purchase an honestly presented animal. (Here's another reason for consulting a previous handler or owner and enlisting the aid of a mentor. An experienced horseman can see through feeble excuses.)

Watch How the Horse Moves

After looking at the animal in the stall, lead him outside to check his gait. Ask the seller or your advisor to hold the lead rope while you check the animal's conformation from the front, back, and each side. Don't ignore the off side, which many people don't really see. Many colic surgeries are performed on the horse's right side, and you could miss the resulting scar. Even with successful surgery, a horse could remain prone to colic for life.

Learn the Medical History

Find out about the animal's medical history. Is he current with shots and worming? Has he suffered from frequent attacks of colic or any other

Where to Search for Your Horse

By choosing a professional or experienced amateur as your mentor, you've enlisted the aid of an insider who knows the market.

Hire a Trainer. A trainer will have especially established a wide range of contacts. She'll be able to research the background of horses in your price range. She knows whom to trust, and she can represent you well by asking those tough questions.

A trainer will want to find you the right horse so you'll remain a customer. She'll also verify that the seller represents the horse fairly, and that any registration papers are in order. It's worth paying a commission or finder's fee for the peace of mind.

A trainer can charge a fee of 5 to 10 percent. Usually the seller pays this, so the trainer quotes you a price that includes the fee.

Buy through Ads. You can also buy a horse through advertisements, sales, or horse dealers. Here you definitely want to bring your mentor along, because every seller has a reason for selling his or her

horse. You don't want to end up with someone else's problem!

Buy at Auction. A horse auction offers a variety of animals for comparison, but comparison shopping demands an expert's eye. It's easy to get "auction fever," especially when you see good-looking horses going for reasonable prices. The impact of the economy has affected sale prices, and you can find a bargain if you shop carefully.

Attend only a reputable auction, such as one affiliated with a breed association or an established sales agent. Such sales will provide a Coggins certificate and proof of registration. Here you'll register with the sales office as a qualified buyer. With your mentor, sort through the catalog for prospects, inspect them, and try out the likeliest candidates.

The consignor may have determined the horse's reserve — the minimum bid. This may be a sealed bid that the auctioneer announces when bidding stops. If you have the highest bid, and the reserve price is higher, either you raise your bid to meet the reserve or you don't buy the horse.

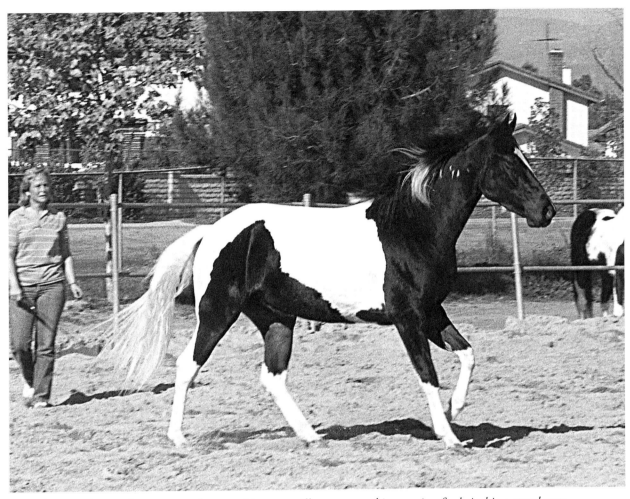

In order to evaluate a horse you are interested in, you will want to see him moving freely in his natural state.

serious conditions? Ask to see the Coggins certificate and other official medical records, preferably from the horse's regular veterinarian. Also ask if the horse is HYPP negative (free of hyperkalemic periodic paralysis). This cell disruption affects thousands of Quarter Horses tracing to the stallion Impressive, and it has spread to horses of other breeds with Quarter Horse ancestry.

While the seller is present, don't criticize the horse. Ask questions, and note any deviations you see. Discuss them with your mentor later. If you decide to buy the horse, you may have your veterinarian perform a formal, professional examination. This could include radiographs and even ultrasound, depending on the horse's value and planned work.

Don't expect to locate a perfect horse, because there aren't any. Weigh the evidence and learn to recognize the obvious faults that will limit a horse's useful life. You're on your way to finding your equine partner, and you'll avoid needless medical bills while saving yourself some heartbreak.

Consider a horse's resale value. Arizona Quarter Horse trainer Casey Hinton has rated these characteristics as important: "Prettiness, bloodlines, conformation, and performance make up the value of a horse. He can be a great mover with good conformation and still win a lot, but not be pretty. The value is higher if he's pretty. You can always sell one that's pretty."

In today's market, the attractive Western horse displays the elegance of Thoroughbred breeding. He doesn't have to resemble a hunter or a stakes winner, but he should show the influence of a slightly longer-legged ancestor.

Component	Detail	Questions to ask yourself
Conformation	Overall balance (see page 20)	Does the horse show breed type? Does he have a short head that shows breed character?
Soundness and Health	Eyes	Does the horse seem to have normal vision? Do you see any infection in either eye?
	Nostrils	Do you see any discharge?
	Mouth	Do teeth meet evenly? Does the breath smell abnormally strong? (The horse could have an abscessed tooth.) Are the gums a normal pink? Check the capillary refill by pressing your thumb against the gum, releasing, and watching how quickly the pink color returns (see page 109).
	Neck	Are ventral muscles overly developed? (The horse could be a cribber.)
	Legs	Is the horse lame? Does the horse move evenly on all 4 legs? Do his joints and bones look strong and powerful? Does the horse have any abnormalities — enlargement or scar — on any leg? Feel inside and outside, front and back, of each leg, and look for unusual heat, or splints, or swellings.
	Hooves	Does the pulse feel strong and normal? (Feel it on the posterior digital blood vessels on the pastern.) Are hooves smooth on the surface?
	Back	Feel for smooth vertebrae on back and withers. Does the horse have strong loins? (Press on the loins to see how the horse reacts to your fingers.)
	Tail	Does the horse move his tail normally? (Grasp the tail to see how the horse moves it.)
	Wind	Does the horse breathe abnormally after exercise at the trot or lope?

Component	Detail	Questions to ask yourself
Temperament	Attitude under saddle	Does the horse feel light and responsive? Will he put up with your riding skills? Is he calm and level-headed? Does he show any bad habits or potentially dangerous behaviors?
	Manners on the ground	Does the horse have soft eyes and a friendly expression? Do you feel confident handling him? Will he load readily into a trailer?
	Movement	Does the horse move smoothly at all gaits? Does his way of going match the riding you plan to do?
Athletic Ability	Moves in balance at all times	Does the horse have light or heavy muscling? Too little or too much can affect his performance. Does the horse move straight? Does the horse react quickly, or does he seem lazy? Does the horse show the courage and heart to perform?
Physical Condition	Muscle tone Strength Endurance	Does the horse's frame appear substantial, rugged, and durable?
	Amount of flesh	Is the horse in good shape, not too fat or too thin? You should be able to just feel the ribs, without them being apparent to the eye.
Affinity	Appeal	Is this horse pretty to look at? Is he fun to be around?
	Color	Do you like his color and markings? If a Paint, Pinto, or Appaloosa, does he have "loud" color?
	Size	Is he the right size for you? Average horse size would be 14.3 to 15.2 hands.
	Presence	Does the horse look alert?

The Balanced Horse

A horse's form definitely influences his function. An equine athlete must display natural balance. His skeletal structure determines how every part fits together — proportions and angles.

Horsemen evaluate the animal's balance by comparing these parts and seeing how the horse ties together. Prominent judge Don Burt has said: "The balance of angulation should be symmetrical and match in all parts, regardless of the animal's size. You could have a horse that is 16.2 hands with the parts of a smaller one — a straight, up-and-down shoulder and a long cannon bone. You want to see a shorter cannon and longer shoulder to get the right relationship between the forearm and pastern."

Burt has also emphasized how the angles influence the horse's movement. He described the balanced horse as standing in a trapezoid. "Look at the angles of the shoulder and hip. If they are equal, the horse will be balanced. A short topline

To Buy or Lease

Buying a horse is a major decision, and it's much easier to buy one than to sell one. If you're serious about horsemanship, realize that your first horse may not be the animal that becomes your genuine partner. California trainer Gill Swarbrick has said: "When you're learning, the horse has to be a machine. You don't necessarily keep your first horse. You're going to make mistakes, and the only way you learn is through making mistakes. Hopefully the horse has the personality that will hold together even through all the mistakes."

One horse may be perfect to start with, but you may want to move on to a specialist or a different type of horse later. Or, your first horse may not be the horse for you.

If you want your own horse but aren't sure about buying one, consider leasing a horse that you can learn on. Your instructor might have an older horse that she doesn't want to sell, but you can have exclusive use of him for a period of time. You can test your riding skills and develop your goals without the permanent commitment to a particular horse.

When leasing a horse, be sure both parties sign a written agreement. The American Quarter Horse Association (AQHA) uses a Lease Authorization form for its members, which proves to the association the lessee's authority. Both owner and lessee sign the authorization. You should follow up a form like this with an agreement that lists specific responsibilities of both parties.

When you are ready to buy, you will note that prices vary, depending on the horse's age, training, potential, and condition. Here are some average starting prices for a trained horse suitable for an amateur or youth rider:

* Unregistered pleasure horse — $500–2,000
* Registered pleasure horse — $2,000–up
* Registered show horse (Pleasure, Horsemanship) — $3,500–up
* Games horse — $2,000–up
* Cutting or reining horse — $5,000–up

Expect some sort of written agreement at the time of sale. You might receive only a handwritten bill of sale for an unregistered horse. With a registered animal, the seller should complete an official transfer form. Usually the seller sends the original registration papers and the transfer to the association, and the association mails you the papers after recording the transfer.

Don't pay the seller until you see that signed transfer form in your hand. You might choose to have the seller sign, and you submit the paperwork to the association. If you're unsure about this process, telephone the secretary of the association for the official procedure.

A balanced horse will have equal angles at the shoulder and hip, as well as a short topline and long underline.

and a long underline complete the trapezoid." (See illustration above.) He adds that both shoulder and hip angles should match in length as well as slope. A horse with one shorter angle, such as a steep shoulder or dropped-off croup, will be off balance. He'll find it difficult to collect himself, to work off the hindquarters.

"If the horse has too much angle in front, and not enough in back, his parts can't work together," Burt explained. "He starts to tire, usually first in the back. The back has to move forward and back for impulsion. The horse loses his impulsion if the rear has to drive more to push the front. When the angles work together, the horse carries a level topline."

Casey Hinton has advised looking at a horse from the withers, the animal's balance point or center of gravity. "This is where he's going to balance himself. The shoulder comes from the withers, so the horse sets his balance. A higher-withered horse is better, because he balances on his hip. The more a horse can do naturally on his hip than on his front, the better he'll be. The horse that floats backwards as he lopes — lopes from his hip — will always be a good mover."

Hinton has said that the longer the neck, the better the horse's natural balance. He can predict a good mover by observing the structure of the neck and the hip. And, according to Don Burt, collection plus impulsion results in balance, whether the horse stands still or moves out. When you study a horse for balance, ask a handler to stand the horse square. He should stand with weight on all four legs placed under his body.

Part	Angle	Proportion
Overall symmetry		Body in thirds of equal proportion: forehand, barrel, hindquarter Length equals height, so horse can carry weight Parts blend together smoothly Muscling appears smooth, with a combination of Quarter Horse and Thoroughbred appearance
Head	Held in a comfortable position	Sized to fit the horse Length related to horse's weight and height
Eyes	Placed on the sides of the head about ⅓ the distance from poll to muzzle	Large Same size
Ears	Erect	Short Alert Same size Sized to fit the head
Jaw		Prominent, well-defined
Muzzle		Well-defined, refined chin
Neck		Long, trim neck for flexibility Defined jugular groove Distance of topline (withers to poll) equals twice the bottom line
Throatlatch		Trim throatlatch Distance from poll to throat measures ½ the length of the head — large enough for an unobstructed airway
Shoulder	Sloped at 45° for a longer stride Should match angle of hip	Big shoulder Long shoulder for a long neck Distance from point of shoulder to haunch equals length of head
Withers		Sharp, prominent Slightly higher than croup for "uphill" appearance that lightens the weight on the forehand
Chest		Sufficient width between the forelegs Broad chest indicates athletic breathing capacity Prominent V-muscling indicates power
Heart girth		Deep for lung capacity Measurement equals length of head and length of foreleg From the side, ribs look well sprung

Part	Angle	Proportion
Foreleg	Placed straight under the horse Forearm forms 90° angle with shoulder Bones run straight into the hoof Viewed from the front, a plumb line can run from the middle of the hoof to the point of the shoulder Horse does not toe in or out Horse does not camp out or behind Horse is not over or back at the knee	Viewed from the front, all parts of both forelegs match from right to left Cannons short so knees are close to ground Long, well-muscled forearm blends into shoulder
Front feet	Pastern and hoof sloped at 45° Stands square on feet Heels are equal	Round shape Sized for the horse Same size Pastern fairly long Pastern forms one slope, not broken for coon foot or club foot
Underline	Smooth curve from girth to flank	Long, measured from elbow to stifle
Hip	Slope matches shoulder's slope (measure from the muscle on the hip, just ahead of the flank, to just above the gaskin) Hip and stifle joints meet at 90°	Powerful source for all gaits Higher set tail indicates length of femur is longer than pelvic bone, for a longer stride Viewed from the side, the hindquarters appear square and wide from stifle to stifle
Hind leg	Viewed from the side, an imaginary line should run down middle of gaskin, hock, hoof From behind, legs don't angle together (cowhocked) or stand too far apart (base wide) Hocks form a 130° angle Hocks aren't too angled (sickle hock) or too straight (post legged)	Cannons short so hocks close to ground Long and strong muscles Stifle blends into hindquarter Prominent muscles in gaskin, but not so heavy that the horse loses flexibility
Topline	Horizontal	Short, not concave (length of back varies; a long-backed horse may still be athletic)
Loin	Horizontal	Wide and strong to carry rider, flexible enough to bend laterally and longtitudinally so horse gets hind end under himself
Hind feet	May toe out slightly Heels equal	Oval shape Same size
Croup	Sloped Top matches or slightly below point of the shoulder, straight across	Long and wide

Gait	Footfalls	Attributes	Faults
Walk	4-beat gait, with no period of suspension 1-2-3-4	Horse moves forward with energy and impulsion, so he covers ground. He flows in a fluid motion, pushing from the hips. He moves flatfooted, places center of hoof on ground. Neck moves flexibly so the horse breathes easily in motion.	Interfering: feet brush or knock each other Hits ground on outside or inside edge of feet, which creates stress on legs
Trot	2-beat gait 1-2	Horse covers ground, definitely moving forward. He trots or jogs smoothly and rhythmically. He trots in cadence, with his opposite feet hitting the ground at the same instant. He can lengthen his stride and keep his impulsion without increasing speed. Topline remains level and the back "round." When turning, the horse rolls his back and drops his head.	Interfering Horse appears rough-gaited, his topline jolting up and down. He raises his head to maintain his balance (a too-high head weakens the back). He trots "strung-out," with too much weight on the forehand. When turning, he hollows his back, raises his head, and bounces.
Lope	3-beat gait 1-2-3 (emphasis on the first footfall)	Level topline Fluid way of going Horse sweeps forward with his hind legs, lifting the forehand. He lopes effortlessly. His front feet land flat, low to the ground.	Horse pounds the ground. He shows excess action at the knee and hock. His topline rolls. He 4-beats, or seems to trot in front and walk behind (listen to the gait to confirm). He moves in a short, choppy lope. The lope looks lateral.
Gallop	3- or 4-beat gait, depending on speed		

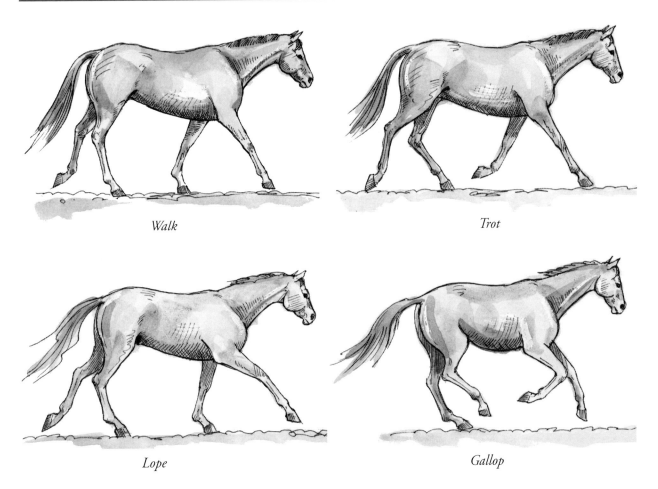

Walk

Trot

Lope

Gallop

Observe the horse being led or longed. Look for smooth, ground-covering gaits that you want to feel from the saddle.

Then watch the horse in motion, being led at the walk and trot, or longed at trot and canter. Look for a good mover, a horse that moves in balance. You're going to ride the horse, so look for smooth gaits that will be comfortable for you for hours at a time.

A horse with correct angles should move cleanly. Watch how he changes gait, turns, and stops. You want to see him maintain his own balance, with or without a rider. For a show horse, he should be a "big stopper," or stop immediately with his hindquarters under himself.

From the side, does the horse move true, with pure gaits? Do you see free shoulder movement, with a soft, swinging back? From the front, does he walk straight? From the rear, does the hind end move smoothly? It shouldn't shift or bounce.

"A horse goes as he is designed to go," according to Burt. "You cannot make a horse with bad angles go as balanced as one with good angles."

Getting Along with Your New Horse

When your new horse moves in, the two of you enter into a new friendship. You'll learn all about his personality, and he'll learn about yours. As you begin to adjust to one another, you'll become acquaintances, and then comrades.

Look for the hock to line up with the point of the buttock. The straight line shows useful structure.

A good foreleg is placed straight under the horse. The horse isn't back at the knee or over the knee.

The front feet should show a pastern sloped at a 45 degree angle. Avoid a foot that's too sloped or too straight, or with a broken angle (club foot).

Expect it to take at least six months for you to understand your horse. He may be used to different handling, and both of you need to explore the other's responses. Like teammates in basketball, you'll learn all your horse's moves so you can mesh into a congenial partnership.

Horses are creatures of habit, and they crave regularity. Change upsets many animals. You'll adjust more rapidly to the horse than he will to you, so don't rush the process. Gradually introduce any changes in stabling, diet, or routine.

Moving can stress your new horse. You can ease his anxiety by allowing some time alone to explore his stall or paddock. If possible, keep curious equine neighbors at a safe distance. Duplicate the horse's previous environment as much as you can, and definitely offer familiar feed. You certainly don't want to trigger an immediate attack of colic!

Watch your horse in the stall or paddock, so you can observe his normal actions. This will help you discern any changes due to ill health or injury.

At home, you might notice your new horse acting differently than he did when you observed him before. Expect unusual behavior as he adjusts to his new home, and don't assume that he'll act predictably.

For example, never turn a new horse into a pasture with an already-established herd. Maybe he lived peaceably with other horses, but the new group requires that he find a place in the pecking order. It's safer to introduce him to one or two others at a time, allowing less hazardous interaction.

You're anxious to start working with your new horse, but let him have some time to adjust before you start handling him. Never just saddle up and set off for a fast ride.

Give both yourself and your horse time to establish harmony by getting to know each other face to face, on the ground.

Trainer Gill Swarbrick rides the new horse for a rider, to find out any idiosyncracies. She can then advise the rider how to deal with him, and to predict what he'll do in any situation. "The horse and rider need to get to know one another, and they can't do that in a high-stress situation. At the beginning, I say, 'Don't try to *do* anything with the horse. Just go out and walk, trot, lope, but don't do anything intense. If you do and you have a fight and you lose, it's going to be harder.'"

Give both yourself and your horse time to establish harmony. First you'll get to know your horse face to face, on the ground. Chapter 3 will help you begin to handle your horse.

Handling Your Horse

ou want the Western horse to be your partner. Riding becomes fun when your horse joins with you. As dominant partner, you dictate his actions. You influence the relationship through your first interactions.

By handling the horse on the ground, you learn how he responds to you before you ride him. Watch his expression to anticipate his reactions to you, other horses, and other sights and sounds in the area. The horse learns about you by observing your body language, your movements, and your emotions.

To enjoy your horse, you must be able to contain him. If you don't control the horse, the horse will control you. At all times, you must supervise the horse's actions. You handle the horse gently but firmly; your goal is to contain him without force.

Trainer Pat Parelli has explained how horses look up to a leader. "Horses are natural followers. Your horse sizes you up. He respects you for your leadership qualities."

Establish yourself as a leader by knowing what you want to do with a horse *before* you start an action. Visualizing your goal helps you carry through, and you will communicate your desire to the horse. You act without threatening him. As you move deliberately around your horse, he'll understand and follow your lead. Your confidence — and kindness — will keep you in control.

Catching the Horse

Few riders today actually catch horses with swinging ropes. A more correct description would be to approach and halter the horse while he remains motionless. Most riders use a halter and lead rope.

A halter contains the horse safely, with a lead rope snapped to the halter's center ring. Drape the unbuckled halter, with the lead rope attached, over your arm or shoulder while you approach the horse in the stall, corral, or pasture. Coil the lead so it doesn't drag on the ground or trip you.

If your horse has proven difficult to catch, you may wish to conceal the equipment behind your back. Walk up to him, stopping at his near (left) shoulder. Pet the shoulder and neck as the horse stands quietly, and gradually ease the halter noseband toward the muzzle. Use both hands to spread open the noseband, and hold it low so the horse is less likely to raise his head. A gentle horse will lower his head to allow you to place the halter.

Haltering the Horse

Gently maneuver the straps of the halter over the muzzle. Slide your left hand along the near cheekpiece, toward the ear, and reach under the throat with your right hand. Grasp the loose end of the halter's crownpiece on the offside, and buckle the two ends of the crownpiece before collecting the lead rope.

You might choose to place the lead rope over or around the neck before you slip on the halter. This won't really hold a horse that tries to bolt away from you, but it can convince the animal that you've caught him.

With a broke horse, some handlers prefer using a neck rope instead of a halter and lead rope. The neck rope has a rope or metal loop in place of a snap. You form a non-slip noose using the metal adjuster. Hold the loop in your right hand and approach the horse's near shoulder. Move your hand under his neck and gently lift the loop over his muzzle and ears. Tighten the loop snug around the neck, which can be a few inches behind the poll or mid-neck.

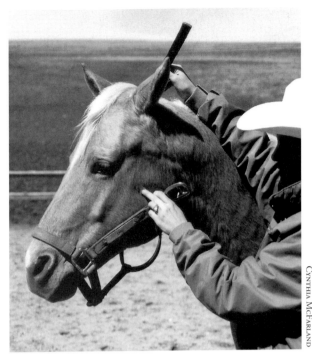

Gently maneuver the strap over the muzzle, bring the loose end of the crownpiece over the poll, and buckle the two ends.

The neck rope can substitute for a halter. The metal adjuster holds the rope so it won't tighten around the horse's throat.

Leading the Horse

With the horse contained, you walk him as you would a dog. You indicate the gait and direction, and the animal moves alongside you as a partner.

Stand on the near side, about one foot away from the horse's shoulder. Place your right hand on the lead rope, six to eight inches from the snap or neck loop, with the rope slack. Hold your arm straight out from your body at a comfortable level.

Gather the rest of the lead rope into coiled loops, and wrap your left hand over — never through — the loops. You can feed out rope if necessary, and if the horse jerks the rope, the coils won't tighten around your fingers or hand. Don't let the end of the lead rope drag on the ground. You or the horse could step on it.

Facing forward, signal the horse to move by striding ahead. The broke horse automatically follows on a slack lead. Rely on your peripheral vision to observe his response. If you look at him, you could distract him.

As you lead the horse through doorways or gates, aim him straight between each side. Don't try to squeeze him through an opening narrower than four feet or he could injure a hip on the post or jamb.

Use caution when the two of you pass a fence, walk down a barn aisle, or pass stable tools. Just when you least expect it, the horse could swish his tail and snag the hairs on a wire fence, get bitten by a stalled horse leaning over the door, or fall over a rake.

The horse should pace his steps to your strides and keep his neck beside your right shoulder. Ideally he maintains a safe distance from your shoulder, hip, and feet.

Don't allow your horse to push forward or lag behind. If you need to turn him, turn him away from you, to the right. Turn the head, and the body will follow.

When you arrive at the hitching rail, stop, which signals the horse to halt. If he doesn't, tug downward on the lead shank and say, "Whoa."

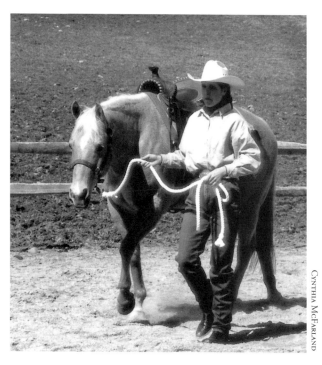

When leading, the horse should pace his steps to your stride, keeping his neck beside your right shoulder. Maintain a safe distance from your shoulder, hip, and feet.

Tying the Horse

Tying is another learned behavior; it contains the horse and curbs his instinct to move. You secure your horse's head to ensure that he remains in one place while you prepare for riding. He should stand tied as long as you decide, whether it's a few minutes or several hours. Usually you knot the lead rope or neck rope to a solid object, so the horse won't get loose.

Pick a safe area, where your horse won't contact any potentially dangerous objects. If other horses are tied nearby, be sure that yours cannot contact his neighbors.

You can use a tie rail, sturdy fence, solid post, tree or stout limb, ring on the side of a horse trailer, or cross ties. Whatever you choose, test it for strength. Will it securely hold a horse that fights the lead rope? If you can budge a post or rail by pushing or lifting it, don't tie your horse to it.

Fit the end of the rope around a rail, allowing 18"–24" in length. Tie a quick release knot as shown. Always check the knot before you walk away.

The cross tie secures the horse with two ropes, one on each side of his head. You can cross tie a horse between two objects — fences, walls of a barn or stall, posts, or trees.

Whether you tie with one rope or two, position the restraint so the horse's head remains in a comfortable position. The rope should not force the head downward or the neck upward, and the knot should remain in place. A rope at the height of the horse's withers is safest, so he won't catch a forefoot over the tie rope.

Fit the end of the rope around a rail or through a tie ring. Allow 18 to 24 inches in length, and tie a knot that you can jerk loose instantly, as illustrated in the diagram. This knot will untie easily, even if your horse pulls against it and tightens the rope.

Check the knot before you walk away. Don't leave the horse unattended unless you know he's broke to tie and won't fight the rope or try to untie it.

When you untie a knot, loosen it by pulling near the end of the rope. Then untie.

Some horses will "ground tie" and wait for their riders to return.

Ground Tying

Some Westerners teach their horses to *ground tie.* Whenever the rider dismounts and drops the reins ahead of the horse, to the ground, the broke horse freezes. He stands in place, waiting for the rider to return.

Those movie cowboys who galloped to the saloon and tossed their reins over the hitching rail were actually ground tying their horses. The "parked" horses were trained to ground tie — the hitching rail was a prop.

Hobbles

Some riders rely on hobbles, which restrain the horse by encircling the two front legs. Hobbles strap the forelegs together at or above the fetlocks. They don't stop a horse from moving, but they restrict his movement.

A short piece of cotton rope forms a simple set of hobbles for a hobble-trained horse. The rope is looped around the off foreleg, twisted a few times, and looped around the near fore. Tie a loose double knot that will not be difficult to unfasten. A cotton rope will not tighten as much as nylon or poly, and it will not burn the skin if the horse pulls against the rope.

After currying, brush off the dirt particles with firm strokes that go with the lay of the coat.

A hobbled horse will usually stand still. Some might "hop" slowly, or even try to gallop, but they usually won't stray very far.

You'd usually restrain a horse with hobbles while trail riding, to keep your horse in camp. If you have a horse trained to hobbles, you don't need to tie him with a rope to groom him. Simply tie rope or feed-sack hobbles, or buckle manufactured hobbles of leather or braided mohair cinch cord. With rope hobbles, stand at the near foreleg and flip the hobble around the off foreleg. Twist the rope a few turns and wrap the near leg. Tie with a square knot, which will hold in place yet untie easily.

Picket Rope

Your horse may be trained to accept a picket rope. Here you attach the horse's halter or neck rope to a long rope, tied to a stake driven into the ground. You can also use a stake-out hobble, in which one strap buckles around a foreleg. A rope snaps to the hobble. The horse can move freely the length of the rope, to graze in a certain area.

Never stake out or hobble a horse unless you are sure the animal is used to these methods. He must accept the restraint. A horse trained to a picket rope knows how to avoid becoming tangled, and knows to stand quietly if he does tangle the rope around his feet.

Groups of trail riders often use the picket line, adopted from the Old West. This is an improvised tie rail made of stretched rope, to which the riders tie their horses overnight or on a long rest stop.

Grooming the Horse

With your horse tied, clean him before you saddle up. Currying massages the skin and coat, while

Regular Grooming

The following grooming chores should be performed regularly.

This handling should be positive and pleasurable for both you and your horse. Most horses learn to enjoy this attention.

* ✯ Rub horse with towel to loosen dirt.
* ✯ Scrub coat with curry comb to lift dirt to the surface.
* ✯ Curry or sponge the face.
* ✯ Brush loosened dirt from the body.
* ✯ Rub coat with soft brush or cloth.
* ✯ Untangle any knots and remove debris from the main and tail.
* ✯ Brush dirt from hoof walls and pick feet.

Use these basic tools for daily grooming: 1. Towel; 2. Curry mitt; 3. Rubber curry comb; 4. Sponge; 5. Sweat scraper; 6. Body brush; 7. Finishing brush; 8. Hoof pick.

brushing strokes the coat to whisk off dirt and loose hair raised by the curry. You can also clean the coat with a rough-textured cloth, either a folded burlap sack or a cactus cloth.

Start at the horse's neck. Stand so you face toward the horse's rear. With a currycomb or cloth, scrub the coat and skin in a circular or back-and-forth motion. Work against the lay of the coat to raise dirt to the surface. Once you've curried both sides of the horse, including back and belly, use a brush to whisk off dirt particles. Brush with firm strokes over the entire body, including the face.

Brush the mane and forelock flat against neck and forehead. Brush the tail, separating strands with your fingers so you don't pull out tail hairs.

As you groom, observe the condition of coat and skin. If your horse has any abrasions or sores, treat them with medication after you finish brushing the coat.

Touching the horse while grooming helps the two of you bond with each other. Most horses enjoy the touch, especially when you rub the coat with a soft brush or the palm of your hand. Watch the horse's facial expression as you groom. Look for favorite spots, and spend extra time rubbing these areas.

The Broke Horse

The first horse you handle should be a gentle "broke" horse. The broke horse allows you to handle him. He accepts your dominance through all contact.

CYNTHIA MCFARLAND

Mutual respect is an important part of the horse and rider relationship.

Through training, the broke horse has learned good habits. Repetition has taught him to respond to any handler. He feels comfortable and he behaves as expected.

You master the animal through your intelligence, as you cannot physically overpower a horse or pony. You reinforce the horse's habitual behaviors by consistent reward and punishment.

Trainer Casey Hinton has said: "The horse is a creature of habit. We teach him the habits, so use the same habits every day."

As you observe horses, you see that they tend to seek the path of least resistance, or a lack of punishment. You reward the horse that leads correctly by not punishing him. You discipline the resistant horse by voice, pressure of the lead rope, or use of a whip. If you allow the horse to do what he wants, you allow him to begin a bad habit. With careless handling, even a broke horse could become rank, behaving dangerously on the ground or under saddle. "Horses are totally subservient to humans," according to Art Gaytan, a California trainer. "The horse should do only what you ask, not what he wants."

Casey Hinton: "What motivates a horse is rest, or food. If you use that to your advantage, a horse will do almost anything for those things. Part of training him is training his mind to think that he's surrendering, giving in to you, because he thinks he'll get rest."

Hinton has defined training as "Command, respect, response." And Gaytan has said: "The secret to training horses is three elements: Ask, put on the pressure that equals the horse's resistance, and reward."

A horseman respects his or her horse and expects respect in return. The horse learns that when he responds to a person's command, he displays and receives respect.

Trainer Terry Berg has described this as boundaries that both parties observe. "The horse has his space, and you have your space. A horse is a big enough animal that he can step on your foot, and it hurts. He can do a lot of damage. If he won't move away from you on the ground easily, or back up, or stay out of your space, you're in trouble."

A Broke Horse

* Has manners, both on the ground and under saddle.
* Gives to the pressure of a strap, rope, hand, or leg.
* Doesn't run away from most threatening sights and sounds.
* Is attentive to you.
* Accepts your dominance and respects you.

Respect doesn't mean fear. The horseman avoids frightening the horse. The horse avoids threatening the person. According to Berg, "The horse shouldn't come out of his boundary and into the person's boundary. That shows the horse is telling the person where the boundary is. That is a real dangerous point."

You're always training a horse, whenever you interact with him. Horses respond differently, and Oregon trainer Tom Sorensen has explained how you can test an equine personality just by leading the horse. "You can have a horse with a hot mind in a hot body, a hot mind in a cold body, a cold mind in a hot body, or a cold mind in a cold body. All horses ride exactly the way they lead. The horse that's always right there, shoulder to shoulder with you, is very trainable. That's the hot mind in the cold body — the horse that you can turn on and off like a light switch."

The broke horse responds through his training, not by instinct. One strong instinct is to push against pressure. The late Jack Baker, a legendary California horseman, said: "The first time you put a halter on a colt, he's going to pull away from the pressure that you put on him. It comes from self-preservation. The system of teaching him to give to pressure is the most important thing, and just about the only thing, you're going to teach him in his lifetime."

Trainers agree that another powerful instinct is flight, to flee from fright. The horse naturally defends himself by running away. Trainer Monty

Roberts said: "The horse is a flight animal. He thinks he should leave when he sees danger."

By learning containment — to stand tied no matter what — the horse overcomes this instinct. But although the broke horse acts predictably most of the time, he may behave differently when in danger. Even a well-trained animal never loses his basic instinct of self-preservation. Any horse will run from danger if he can. This animal can injure you when you try to help him, or even himself as he struggles to flee.

Working around horses is risky, so consider a horse to be potentially volatile. Don't become obsessed about what might happen, but be aware of the animal's inherent nature. An accident can happen at any time. As a horseman, you'll scan the environment for a possible hazard. You won't be able to prevent all accidents, but you can prepare yourself to react if necessary.

Equine Language

Whenever you handle a horse, you "speak" to him. All your moves speak to the horse in his language.

To enjoy being around horses, you must adapt to their language. You learn to speak it by learning to "be" a horse, instead of thinking like a human.

This speech is the language of respect, of dominance and submission. You act to control the horse, as another horse would. Your horse submits to your actions, and you reward him by "going submissive." You're copying the behavior of two horses, with your horse submitting to the dominant one, you. He wants to follow you, because you've communicated in a language he can understand.

Master horsemen have learned this language, and some of them teach it to their fellow humans. Trainer Monty Roberts has demonstrated how his body language communicates to the horse. His moves encourage the horse's response. "With communication and kindness, I can get him to want to go with me, rather than to go away."

Roberts works the green horse in a round pen. The horse starts out by running in a circle, then gradually comes to the center to stand still. The

trainer rewards him by letting him stand still when he cooperates. He becomes submissive, turning his back to the horse. When the horse "argues" with the trainer, the trainer takes command and causes him to return to running the circle.

"He decides to renegotiate a contract, to join up with me," said Roberts. "He talks to me in the language 'Equus,' which is 75 million years old. He joins with me as soon as he knows it's good to be with me."

Roberts has communicated with over 7,000 unbroke horses, speaking to them to gain their confidence and trust. When horse and man can communicate, the horse will accept unfamiliar handling.

In the same vein, trainer Art Gaytan has explained how horses understand a different language. "I never talk to horses in my language, but always in their language. A horse's language is 98

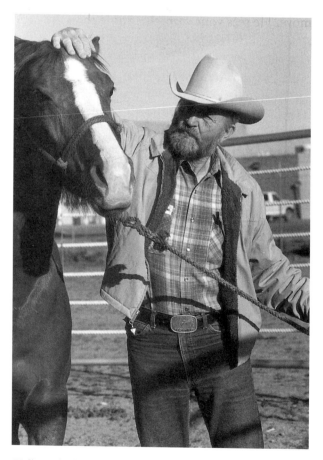

Talk to the horse in his language. Soft actions can ease tense situations.

percent through his eyes, and 2 percent through sound."

The horse's eyes and ears work together. A horse turns his head to look, to focus on a sight. His ears also tell where he looks, as he can see in two directions at once. One ear may turn toward you, while the other indicates that the horse also observes another distraction.

Roberts has pointed out how the horse speaks with eyes, ears, and mouth. As the horse watches a human, his inside ear (the one closest to the person) remains fixed on the person. He demonstrates his submissive response by lowering his head.

Trainer Pat Parelli: "Body language is universal with all beings. A horse with his head up is defensive. Down, he's relaxed. Licking his lips shows he understands, he's digesting a thought. You look for that final understanding, to see his eyes and ears look a little different, for him to lick his lips."

A horse perceives slight changes in the way you move. He sees your mental attitude through your physical attitude. You don't have to make broad moves to elicit the desired response. You should control and soften your actions.

Gaytan has explained how the horse's eyesight affects its thinking. "What a horse sees with his left eye, he doesn't recognize when he sees it with the right eye. The horse has two separate sides of his brain, and he can't transfer information from one eye [side of the brain] to the other."

For this reason, realize that a horse should become used to objects and movement on both sides. You need to mirror your actions left and right. For example, your horse may be accustomed to you holding a whip on its near side. Move to the off side, and the same whip could spook him. Let him see the whip on both sides so he learns to recognize the object.

Horses respond to the handler's movements, according to Gaytan: "Your motion cues a horse when you lead him. The rope is only to keep the horse from running off, because you can't pull him along."

Even though horses focus on your body language, you can enhance your control with your voice. Some experts recommend regular conversation, humming, or whistling.

You can soothe a nervous animal or discipline one with your voice. If you sense a horse might kick, a sharp "Quit!" often corrects his misconduct.

If you find yourself in a tense situation on the ground, re-establish your dominance with your body language and voice. Stop your movement, take a breath, and say "whoa" to freeze the action.

You might use the Tellington-Jones Equine Awareness Method (TTEAM), developed by Linda Tellington-Jones. TTEAM can change the horse's personality. The TTouch bodywork reduces his tightness and sensitivity by relaxing him. Specific touches on the head encourage him to lower his head. TTEAM ground exercises help him to overcome fear and listen to your guidance.

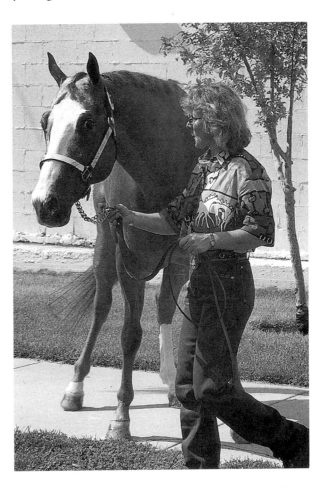

Stay aware of your position and any possible hazards. Tune in to your horse's body language. Let him know when he starts to invade your personal space.

Setting Up an Ideal Horse Enclosure

In the Old West, few horses lived inside barns. Most ranged in huge pastures or in corrals near the ranch. Today's Western horse can live in a backyard pen, a barn, a field, or ranch land. You can choose among facilities, depending on your preference and circumstances. In his enclosure, the horse needs food, water, and shelter.

Every horse must eat and drink to survive, but the type of shelter depends on the local climate and his needs. A pleasure horse may not require a full-scale barn; a simple roof or three-sided shed will protect him from weather extremes.

The enclosure must contain the horse safely. Barbed wire, the fence that changed the West, confines cattle more safely than horses. A horse snagged in barbed wire can fight and injure himself severely. Safer fences for Western horses include metal pipe, wood post and rails, and woven wire. Your horse might respect "hot wire," or electric fencing.

Keep your horse safe by horse-proofing your barn and enclosures. Try to anticipate every possible hazard.

The footing should never be slippery; always remove any poisonous plants; and secure the door to the feed room. Check the heights of ceilings and overhangs. Eliminate any electrical hazards, and see that all gates and doors close tightly. Dispose of trash regularly.

JUNE CAMPBELL

Safe, Defensive Handling

Veterinarians note that most accidents occur during handling — leading, tying, grooming, medicating, and trailer loading. On the ground, you are vulnerable to four common injuries: getting kicked, stepped on, bitten, or shoved. You can protect yourself by expecting that injury. Stand away from any possible danger, let the horse know your location, and tune into his body language.

The typical Western horse or mule weighs 1,000 to 1,400 pounds. Even a pony weighs about 600 pounds. Its very size makes the horse a formidable animal, so apply the 4 A's: Alert and Assertive Avoids Accidents. Here's a checklist of safety guidelines:

1. Avoid standing directly in front of a horse. Every horse will spook. If he strikes or leaps forward, can you jump out of the way quickly? Be alert for any sudden movement. For example, realize that irritating insects can cause him to throw his head, smacking you by accident.

2. Develop "eyes in your feet" whenever you walk near or beside a horse. Keep your two feet at least 12 inches away from all four hooves. While grooming or saddling, stand in a forward-leaning posture. Lean toward the horse instead of standing too close beside him.

3. Always wear protective shoes or boots. A thick rubber, vinyl, or leather boot gives you some cushion against an unexpected stomp. Heed an equine Murphy's Law: The one day you *don't* swap tennis shoes for boots, your horse will plant a hoof right on your toe.

4. Always inspect your equipment's condition. A frayed strap or rope can break if that 1,000-pound horse jerks against it. Metal hardware is the weakest part of your halter and lead rope. Name-brand tack should use better metal parts, which are less likely to break under stress.

5. Instead of a steady pressure, use a pull and release. Think of the lead rope as a rubber band.

Any horse can revert to his instinct to fight pressure. You can't overpower a horse by outpulling him.

If a horse shoves you with his head, shoulder, side, or hip, shove him right back and make him quit or move over with a verbal reprimand, "Get over!"

6. Make your horse respect your space when you're close beside him. If he crowds you when leading or won't stand still when tied, correct him with voice and a slap. "Quit!" or "Stand!" can discourage this movement, which can endanger you and others around your horse.

7. Watch every rope and strap whenever you handle a horse. Many old-time horse trainers are

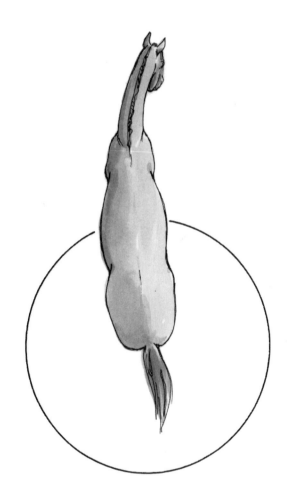

Imagine a semicircle about four feet out from the horse's hindquarters. When you enter that "kicking zone," be assertive, keep body contact, and watch the horse's legs.

missing finger joints from becoming entangled in a rope. Never wrap a rope around your finger or hand, and keep your feet away from a rope loop or a dangling lead rope.

A horse that becomes entangled in a rope can panic. Always keep a sharp pocket knife in the barn or trailer to cut through the rope in an emergency. You can cut the rope to release a struggling horse. (Stay out of the way, because he could bolt when he feels the pressure released.)

8. Kicking poses the greatest danger. The power of the equine hoof can kill you, and every equine can kick. Avoid a kick by simply staying out of the way. Imagine a semicircle, about four feet out from the horse's hindquarters. When you must enter this zone, move close to the horse's side. If he does kick, you'll receive only a shove, not the full force of the kick.

You can avoid a possible kick by reminding the horse of your presence. Pull down on his tail, or keep contact with your hand, shoulder, or leg.

Some animals cowkick, kicking forward or even sideways with the hind leg. Again, draw an imaginary circle around the kicking zone. Keep yourself out of danger, except when you must handle the hindquarters or belly. Enter the zone assertively, keep body contact, and watch the legs.

Don't underestimate the kicking zone. A short-coupled horse or pony can cowkick you when you bend over to pick up a forefoot. Keep an eye on the hind leg when you clean a front hoof on the same side. Your pony might kick forward at a fly on his belly, striking your head!

Whenever a horse kicks, correct him immediately. This is an attack, so never tolerate kicking. Let him know you won't accept this threat. And it doesn't matter if you weren't the intended target — a kick can kill you whether the horse meant to kick you or another victim.

Feet endanger you even when the horse lies down. Stay out of the way when he rolls and kicks all four legs in the air. If he becomes caught in the stall or under a fence, be careful when you help him

regain his feet. In his excitement, he can kick you by accident.

When you bend down or squat to groom the horse's feet or lower legs, keep an eye on the opposite foot. He can lift a foot to knock off a fly and hit you by accident.

9. When you groom a horse, watch his expression. Some horses are ticklish on legs or belly, or around their ears, and they will warn you by moving away, pawing, or threatening to bite or kick. Handle these areas gently so the horse tolerates your touch. Discipline him whenever he resists handling, with a sharp word or slap. Sternly correct a horse that bites or kicks, and watch closely for a repetition of the threat.

10. Prevent accidental nips by holding your hand flat and fingers together when you feed a treat or touch a horse's nose. Few horses bite out of meanness, but some will nip in play. Those big teeth can break bones, so correct this misbehavior immediately.

To feed a horse treats, hold your hand flat with fingers together.

Dealing with Misbehavior

Pat Parelli has said: "Respect is hard to get, but easy to lose. It takes discipline, energy, and maintenance to get."

Not every horse will respect you. If he learned bad habits through careless handling, you'll have to outsmart him in order to catch, lead, and tie him safely.

Horsemen appreciate animals they can catch easily. The opposite horse — one who sidles away and evades capture — can be one of the most frustrating creatures.

Some horses will move their heads to avoid the halter. Worse is the one who continues walking away from you, not allowing you to get close enough to touch him.

Don't chase the horse to make him run. You can try bribing him, luring him close to you. Shake a few oats in a bucket, and allow him to eat. Contain him by encircling the lead rope, or a neck rope, around his neck a few inches behind the throat, and secure the halter.

What if your horse refuses to fall into your trap? You can "walk him down," just following him at a walk until he gives up. Then reward him with grain, pet him, and let him go. This retrains him

through a pleasant experience.

You can also guide the horse into a "ketch pen," or confined area. Even with a hard-to-catch horse, avoid leaving a halter on him. Grabbing the halter can be dangerous, as the horse could drag you if your hand is caught in the straps. Or the horse could snag the halter on a fence, tree, or his own hoof, causing him to panic. (Leave only a break-away halter on a loose horse.)

When you lead him, he might lag behind or charge forward. Tap his hindquarters with a whip in your left hand to urge him forward. Restrain the eager horse with a chain lead shank, fitting the chain over his nose. If he tries to lean into you, slap his shoulder and tell him, "Get over."

If he refuses to walk forward beside you but stares at an object, let him stand and look at whatever has caught his attention. Don't allow him to move away from it, but let him think while he stands in place. Give him time, watch his expression, and then cue him to walk forward again.

If you know your horse fights being tied, don't tie him to a solid object. You can discourage the "halter puller" by tying him to an inner tube wrapped around a tie rail, or a strong stretchy lead rope. The tube or rope will stretch under pressure, then steadily pull the horse back to the rail. The horse learns to keep the rope slack to avoid pressure. A training halter also discourages the horse from pulling against the rope.

If you're new to horses, don't endanger yourself by dealing with one that tries to hurt you. Seek expert training help. A few sessions with a seasoned professional can cure many bad habits.

The best way to learn how to handle horses is to observe an experienced horseman. Watch your instructor, trainer, equine practitioner, or farrier. See how he approaches a horse, and copy his attitude and actions.

4-H horse leaders and many college continuing education classes teach horsemanship and safe procedures. Also, expert horsemen teach their own clinics, open to the public. Authorities such as Monty Roberts, Pat Parelli, John Lyons, Ray Hunt, and Art Gaytan often teach basic horse handling in public settings. In TTEAM sessions, you can learn this approach to working with the horse without force.

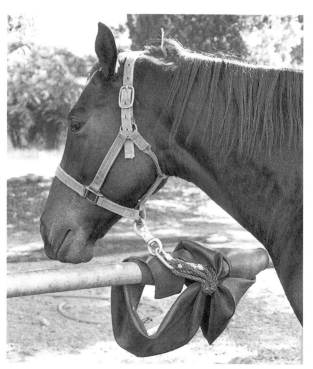

You can discourage a "halter puller" by tying him to an inner tube wrapped around a tie rail. The tube will stretch, then pull the horse back to the rail.

Tacking Up

ow it's time to saddle and bridle your horse so you're ready to ride. As a responsible horseman, you can make riding safer and more pleasurable by following a regular procedure. Choose correctly fitted equipment, and place it on your horse with care. You'll also want to select comfortable Western attire for your hours in the saddle.

Ensuring a Good Fit

No matter how carefully you saddle your horse, the wrong tack can irritate the animal. As the pad and girth press against skin, muscle, and bone, the constant pressure can cause unnecessary discomfort and even pain. Many animals learn to resent their tack during saddling and riding. They demonstrate their discomfort by nipping, kicking, bucking, or even running away.

First, check your saddle to be sure that its tree conforms to the shape of your animal's withers and back. Look for the tree to clear the withers sufficiently. When you sit in the saddle, you should be able to fit two or three fingers between the gullet (under the pommel) and the withers.

Test a new or used saddle before you buy it. Many sellers and tack shops will assist you in checking a saddle on your horse. Evaluate the fit both from the ground and while mounted — just a few minutes will let you know if this is the right tack for your particular horse.

The saddle pad is an important component. With a Western saddle, the pad protects the saddle's wool lining from sweat. It should feel firm, not limp. A pad will measure from one-half to one inch thick. The material should absorb sweat and wick moisture away from the back.

You can choose a pad (a thick square of felt or fleece) or a blanket, or both. Generally, you place a pad next to the horse. On top, follow tradition with a Navajo blanket of woven wool. The blanket covers the pad as a colorful decoration.

Choose tack that fits your horse correctly. Ill-fitting tack can irritate him, and he may learn to resent it during saddling and riding.

Don't expect pads to make a saddle fit your horse. A pile of thick pads can't really cushion the wrong-size saddle, and they can irritate your horse by increasing pressure on the withers. A therapeutic pad can dissipate pressure more evenly, although the permanent solution is matching the saddle tree to the horse's back.

The cinch should fit the horse, too. Usually measuring about 34 inches long, the cinch should not be too long or short, for both comfort and safety. Cinch rings should rest behind and well above the horse's elbows, positioned from 6 to 14 inches below the rigging, depending on the size of horse and saddle. If the rings sit too close to the rigging, you'll have to wrap the latigo once or twice more. Rings that are too low, on a short cinch, will rub the tender skin behind the elbows.

Your saddle is only as secure as your cinch. Never use a cinch that's frayed or rotten. A mohair cinch will be strong and soft against the horse, or you might choose one of the new neoprene models. Use a cinch with rings of brass, bronze, or stainless steel.

For safety, you can now equip a Western saddle with breakaway stirrups. If you or your horse

The saddle's gullet sits above the withers. Cinch rings on this horse are at the right position.

falls, the stirrup releases under the pressure and your foot slips free.

Bridle Parts and Types

You can choose from a variety of bridles, also called "headstalls." Many Western headstalls are doubled and stitched. The leather straps consist of two layers, stitched together for durability and to prevent stretching.

For pleasure and schooling, you can use any style of bridle, of plain or tooled leather, nylon webbing, or plaited nylon cord. Most of these are ½ to ¾ inches wide.

Western reins are of three types: open, closed, or roping. The open, or split, rein is the most common, consisting of two separate straps, ⅜ to 1 inch wide and 6 to 8 feet long. They're made of flat or braided leather, braided mohair, plaited nylon cord, or nylon webbing.

The closed rein is actually three parts. Two reins connect to each other by a three-foot-long romal, or quirt. This style is also called the "California," since it originated with the vaqueros of that state. It's still most often used by West Coast riders, and those who show Arabians or Morgans. The rein and romal can be made of flat or rounded leather, or braided leather or rawhide. The braided styles attach to the bit with snaps or with the self-locking bit ends.

Contest riders often use the roping rein, one continuous strap from 6 to 8 feet long. With no loose ends, the rider can't drop the rein while working. It's made of leather or nylon webbing, and the leather style may be braided in the center for better grip.

A traditional hackamore, which uses a bosal (noseband of plaited rawhide) with a mecate (tied horsehair reins), is unique to Western riding. With it, you use a pull and slack motion, exerting leverage against the horse's nose and lower jawbone.

	Type	Varieties	Uses
METAL MOUTHPIECE OF IRON OR STEEL	Snaffle	O-ring D-ring Twisted wire	Basic bit for schooling and everyday riding Direct action
	Gag	Snaffle Shanked	Timed events, for training and correction Mouthpiece has sliding action
	Curb	Grazing bit Loose-shanked bit	Basic Western bit for a trained horse Used in all types of riding Leverage action A curb with a jointed mouthpiece is a very severe bit.
BITLESS BRIDLE	Hackamore	Bosal Rawhide noseband	Schooling a colt
	Mechanical hackamore	Flat nosepiece Rounded nosepiece Hackamore gag combination	Roping Timed events Pleasure riding Distance riding
	Sidepull	Nylon rope noseband	Schooling a colt

Because bridles are adjustable, you'll find a limited choice in sizes. You can select from pony, Arab, and horse, or full size. If your horse's head seems to be in between, measure the distance from the corner of one lip, over the poll, and to the other lip corner. Compare this measurement with the bridle you're considering, so you're sure it will fit your horse.

Choosing a Bit

Western bits developed from the styles introduced by Spanish horsemen. First forged of iron, bits later became popular in styles manufactured of steel or aluminum. Most contemporary bitmakers produce bits of stainless steel, although horsemen claim that a sweet iron mouthpiece is superior. Quality bits may feature cheeks of stainless steel, for an attractive appearance, and a sweet iron mouthpiece. The iron will rust, but horses seem to prefer the flavor over steel. Many bits also feature copper, either inlaid in iron or steel or as a coating that forms the entire mouthpiece. Proponents feel that both sweet iron and copper encourage the horse to produce saliva. A moist mouth is more responsive to the movement of the bit.

Riders of the West consider the bit a valuable tool for producing a schooled horse. The finished horse performs on a loose rein, wearing a curb bit in the Spanish tradition. Whether the bit is of the Texas (grazing bit) or California (loose-shanked) style, the trained horse responds to a light touch on the reins.

The curb bit operates on leverage, created by the pressure between the mouthpiece and the curb strap or chain. Its severity is influenced by the ratio between the shank above and below the mouthpiece. It must include a curb strap or chain, which

Snaffle bit

Curb bit

Mechanical hackamore

Sidepull

Gag bit

Hackamore

Using a Bitless Bridle

Unique to Western riding is the traditional hackamore bridle, using a bosal with a mecate. The bosal, a noseband of plaited rawhide, is an effective control device. It exerts leverage against the nose and the lower jawbones. The heel knot at the bottom of the bosal adds balance, so the bosal swings free when you slacken the mecate, or tied horsehair reins.

The vaquero used the hackamore as a training device, to school a colt in the basics. He eventually put the colt "in the bridle," progressing to the curb bit.

The hackamore requires a particular kind of touch. You use a pull and slack motion, pulling only one rein at a time. You must know how much strength to apply, and when you need to lighten up the pressure on the horse's sensitive nose and jaw.

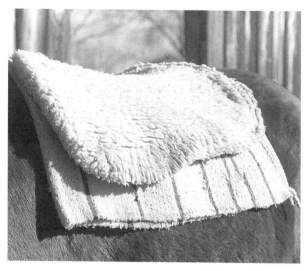

Here, the blanket is placed next to the horse, and the pad is placed on top.

also affects the bit's action through its adjustment. The mouthpiece shape helps the bit to position comfortably on the horse's bars (gums) and tongue.

Your hands make a bit soft or painful. A horseman learns to use any bit with tact, exerting just enough pressure to cue the horse.

Before You Saddle

Most experts agree that you should tie your horse for saddling. He might spook while you connect the cinch, then run off with the saddle sliding off his back. This situation could terrify the horse and cause a serious accident.

With the horse tied to a rail or in crossties, groom his coat to remove all dirt. Pay close attention to the areas that the saddle will touch — withers, back, girthline, and belly. Stretch up to curry and brush the top of the withers, and squat down to clean the belly.

As you groom, check the withers, back, sides, and belly for swellings or scrapes. If you notice a large swelling or break in the skin, treat the area immediately and skip riding for the day. The weight of you and your tack could cause a gall, which will be even more difficult to treat. Galls often cause the white "saddle marks" you see on many horses' withers and backs.

You might choose to saddle the horse anyway, protecting the swollen or scraped skin. You can cushion the cinch with a fleece cover over the strap. Or, if the spot is located on the withers or back, cut a hole in the saddle pad over that place. Ideally, the hole will keep weight from pressing directly over the problem area.

Inspect saddle and pad for safety and cleanliness. Never use a cracked latigo or stirrup leather, or a frayed cinch. Turn over saddle and pad to check the undersides for cleanliness. Remove any burrs or other sharp objects that could irritate the horse's skin.

Placing the Saddle

Traditionally, you saddle from the horse's left (near) side, but your horse should accept saddling from either side. Some people find it more convenient to saddle Western style from the off side. You only have to lift the latigo with the near-side stirrup, instead of the entire length of the cinch, which you leave buckled to the offside billet, or strap.

Place the saddle gently on the pad with the stirrup over the horn.

Whichever side you choose, stand slightly behind the horse's shoulder, with your shoulder about 12 inches away. This position makes it difficult for the horse to bite or kick you. It helps to have "eyes in your feet," which will keep your toes safe from a front hoof.

You'll always use a pad or blanket under a Western saddle. Position the pad partly over the withers, then slide it onto the horse's back, leaving the first inch or so over the withers. By sliding with the hairs, the pad lays the coat flat for a comfortable fit. If you use two blankets or a pad with a blanket on top, hold both as one unit as you place them on the back.

Lift the pad slightly above the bone of the withers. This allows air circulation along the horse's back after you add the saddle.

The pad folds along the center of the horse's backbone. Position the fold so each half of the pad covers an equal portion of the back. Walk around to check from the front or rear and the other side.

Pick up the saddle and arrange stirrups and cinch away from the saddle's underside. Most peo-

ple hang one stirrup over the horn, and the latigo or cinch over the seat.

Next, carefully lift the saddle over the horse's back and set it in place. Never throw it onto the horse. The sudden weight could surprise him, and he could kick or step on you. You also could cause him to cringe and drop his back. If you repeat this thoughtless behavior, he can become "cold-backed." You'll make future saddlings much more difficult, as he retaliates against abuse.

The Western saddle is heavy, and you might not be able to lift it high enough. In this case, lightly swing the saddle onto the horse, using momentum to help you raise and place it.

Position the saddle where it naturally fits behind the shoulder blades. The cinch will hang about 4 inches behind the point of the horse's elbow. If the saddle looks too far forward, slide it slightly back. You may need to move the pad as well, or lift the saddle to move it separately.

If your saddle sits too far back, don't scoot it forward without lifting the pad above the back. If

Run the latigo down and up through the cinch ring.

Once the cinch is tightened, it should fall 6 to 14 inches below the rigging, depending on the size of the horse and saddle.

Never use a cinch or latigo that is frayed or rotten. A traditional mohair cinch is both strong and soft. Cinch rings should be made of brass or stainless steel.

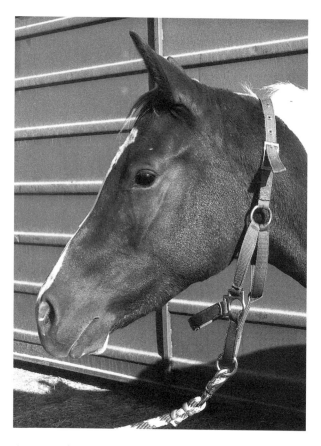

To control your horse while you put the bridle on, buckle the crownpiece of the halter around the neck.

you don't, the movement ruffles the hairs of the coat. This could cause the weight of you and the tack to make sores on the horse's back.

Securing the Saddle

Don't spend too long arranging gear before you secure the cinch. The saddle is merely resting in place, and an abrupt movement could dump it onto the ground.

Quickly make sure that the pad is lying smoothly against the horse's back. If you need to, lift the front again to maintain an air channel. Walk around to the off side to verify that all parts of the saddle and pad lie flat. If you've left the cinch over the seat, carefully lower it. Try not to let the buckle swing against the horse. Back on the near side, loop the stirrup over the horn to uncover the latigo.

Securing the cinch can be the most hazardous part of saddling. Some horses will express their resentment by trying to nip or kick. Protect yourself by scanning the horse's expression, and also keep an eye on his feet. Be prepared to chastise him with a sharp word or slap.

Instead of using a buckle on a cinch ring, you can knot the latigo through the ring on the saddle. Shown are two knots.

Bend over slightly to reach underneath the belly for the end of the cinch. As you place yourself in this dangerous location, keep an eye on the horse. It might help to touch his shoulder with your free hand; you can feel any movement.

Some martingales and breastplates slide over the cinch. If your cinch needs to fit through a connecting strap, attach the tack now, before you buckle the cinch. When you lift the cinch, you'll position the connecting strap mid-belly.

Bring the end of the cinch up toward the latigo. It is best to shorten the strap slowly and smoothly. Your horse will appreciate the gentlest pressure possible, and you'll avoid making him "cinchy."

The large buckle on the cinch fits through holes on the latigo. You will loop the latigo down through the buckle's metal ring, up to the rigging, and down again to fit the buckle's tongue into a hole in the latigo. A short free end of the latigo can hang down from the rigging, or you may run it through a loop strap on the saddle's pommel. Pull the latigo down solidly, so the tongue fits securely into the hole.

You can also secure the latigo by tying a knot instead of using the cinch buckle. When you snug the cinch, check that the skin and hair under it lie flat, with no pinching. You might lift each foreleg up and forward, to eliminate any wrinkles of the skin under the cinch.

Also compare both sides of the cinch rings. Each should reach to the same height on the horse's sides, for equal pressure.

Preparing the Bridle

With the saddle in place, you're ready to replace the halter with the horse's bridle. Your goal is to handle the tack deftly, while gently guiding the animal's head into the headstall.

Before you start, pick up the bridle by the crownpiece to check all parts for safety and cleanliness. Look for any cracked or torn places, especially where the metal or nylon contacts metal hardware. Examine where the cheekpieces attach to the bit. Your bridle will probably connect to the bit with either Chicago screws, buckles, or leather ties. These fasteners must hold the bit securely.

If you haven't used this particular bridle before, check its style. Western bridles fit onto the horse's head with an earpiece or browband and throatlatch. The earpiece holds the bridle around an ear. A split-ear bridle is a crownpiece with a long split in the leather through which the horse's right ear fits. Variations are the shaped-ear and sliding ear. The browband is a strap that attaches across the horse's brow, below the ears and above the eyes. Another strap, the throatlatch, secures the bridle under the jaws and against the throat.

Wash the bit if it's encrusted with dried saliva or feed, and check its condition. A bit can break or wear out. Never use a bit that has cracks or sharp edges, because the metal could injure the horse's lips, tongue, or bars.

Holding the bridle by the crownpiece, arrange the reins in your other hand, or drape them over your shoulder. Shake the bridle so the weight of the bit pulls the straps to hang vertically. This should disentangle any twists in the cheekpieces.

In cold weather, warm the bit just before you ride. You can breathe on the chilled metal, or rub it between your hands.

Placing the Bridle

Always bridle from the near side. You'll adjust the throatlatch or curb strap from that side, and your horse has been trained on that side.

Maintain an alert attitude as you bridle. You place yourself in an awkward, possibly hazardous position, close to the horse's forehand. You have to juggle halter, tie rope, bridle, and reins. Some clever horses have learned to wriggle free during this task.

Standing next to your horse, unfasten the halter and slide it off his nose. Keep the halter against his neck while you rebuckle the crownpiece around the neck. This allows you to control the animal in the moments before you slip the bridle over his ears.

Keep a calm, purposeful attitude when bridling your horse. Pick up the bridle's crownpiece in one hand. (You might choose to drape it over your shoulder, so you can quickly grab it when you remove the halter.) With your other hand, place the

CYNTHIA McFARLAND

CYNTHIA McFARLAND

▲ To fit the bridle, move your right shoulder near the horse's throat. Hold the crownpiece in your right hand, and the mouthpiece in your left palm. Bring the crownpiece close to the horse's forehead and reach it up toward the ears, while you guide the bit into the mouth.

▲ You can modify the basic bridling method if you are short or your horse is tall. Reach your right hand under the horse's neck. Grasp the bridle together and raise it up toward the forehead. With your left hand, slip the bit into the horse's mouth. Now both hands are free to continue.

CYNTHIA McFARLAND

◄ After the bit is in place, both hands are free to move the crownpiece over the ears. With the left hand, slide the crownpiece over the forehead, and with your right hand, gently flick the ears forward at the base as you fit the crownpiece in place. Reach over the poll to fit the off side first. With a tall horse, you will have to do this by feel. With an earpiece, slide the right ear into the slot or loop.

reins over the horse's head to rest partway down the crest. If he starts to move, you can restrain him with both the reins and the buckled halter.

Whichever method you use to hold the bridle as you bring the bit into the horse's mouth, be sure to keep the crownpiece raised with your right hand. If you let it slip down, the horse might open his mouth and drop the bit. The upward pressure of the crownpiece helps keep the bit in place while you fit the bridle behind the ears. Be careful not to force the bit against the horse's lips and teeth. As you pull the crownpiece upward, your left hand will merely point the bit in the right direction. Stretch a finger or two to keep the curb strap underneath the bit, out of the horse's mouth.

Reach under the crownpiece or earpiece to smooth back any loose mane hairs. If the bridle has a browband, pull the forelock over the strap. With a throatlatch, attach it by threading the short top strap down through the buckle on the long strap hanging from the offside. Connect the buckle so the straps lie flat and somewhat loose. You should be able to slide four fingers between the strap and the horse's jaw.

Most horses will cooperate and open their mouths. Yours might choose to evade the bit by clenching his teeth or moving his head. Encourage him to open his mouth by sliding your left thumb or a finger between the lips, into the toothless space on the bars. He should respond by chewing, so slide your finger out as you slip the bit between the parted teeth.

Respect your horse by sliding the bit gently into position. Never shove the bit against the lips or teeth, which can train him to evade bridling.

If he does raise his head high, lips pressed tightly, remain patient yet determined. Urge him to drop his head as you carefully bring the bit into position. Time the insertion of your finger into the mouth so you can quickly move the crownpiece up and the bit in place.

As a last resort, you might wipe a dab of molasses or peanut butter on the bit's mouthpiece. Resorting to this enticement might save some time, while it rewards (and hopefully retrains) the ornery horse.

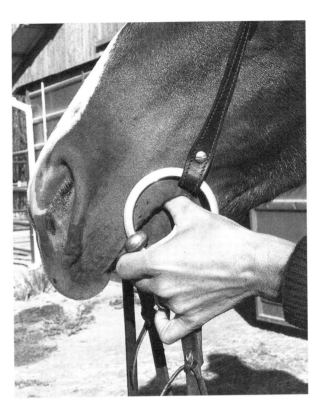

Insert your thumb between the lips to encourage the horse to open his mouth. This headstall uses Chicago screws at the bit ends. Check them often to be sure they are still secure.

A better way to soothe the head-shy horse is to rub the sides of the horse's mouth and ears. Soothe him by gentle massage with your left hand, as you hold the bridle in place with your right. Drop your left hand to the bit, and easily "swoop" the bit into the horse's open mouth.

Carefully place the crown behind the ears. Flick them gently from the base, without bending them. Reach over the poll to fit the offside portion first. If your horse is tall, you'll have to do this by feel. With an earpiece, slide the right ear into the slot or loop.

Bridle Adjustment

Look for all straps to rest flat against the horse's face. The browband should rest close to the ears. Cheekpieces should position the bit snugly, not too tight or too loose. A *curb bit* fits into the corners of the mouth without forming any wrinkles there. Adjust the buckle on the nearside cheekpiece to raise or lower the bit. If you have to adjust it more than one hole, move to the off side to shorten or tighten that cheekpiece. Ideally the buckles sit the same distance from the bit on both sides, so the bridle fits evenly.

The curb strap should hang so you can fit one or two fingers under it when the reins are slack. Test the strap's action by pulling back on the reins. As the bit's shanks move back toward the saddle, the strap should exert pressure. Release the reins, and the shanks swing freely forward.

A *snaffle bit* should fit right into both corners of the mouth, forming one wrinkle on each side. Don't make the bit fit too tightly, with two wrinkles, or too low. A horse can put his tongue over a loosely fitted snaffle.

With the bridle adjusted, remove the halter from around the horse's neck.

To check the length of your stirrups, hold the base of the stirrup against your armpit. Stretch the leather along the underside of your arm. Your fingertips should touch the top of the leather, where it attaches to the saddle tree.

Ready to Ride

Just before you mount, check saddle and bridle for security. Tighten the cinch so it's snug but not overly tight.

If you have to shorten it quite a bit, space the tightenings over two or even three times. Many horses have learned to combat the compression by holding their breath, which forces you to readjust the girth several times. You can combat this by prodding the horse to exhale, using your knee against his belly.

With your saddle in position, you're almost ready to mount. You might want to check the length of your stirrup leathers, to gauge that they're adjusted correctly. Hold the base of the stirrup against your armpit so you stretch the leather along the underside of your arm. Your fingertips should touch the top of the leather, where it attaches to the saddle tree.

Use the stirrup buckle to adjust the length of the leathers. Unfasten the top section of the metal buckle by sliding it upward. Lower or raise the lower section to fit into a different pair of holes in the leather. Lower the top section so it clicks back over the lower part, fastening the buckle securely in place.

Count the number of rows of holes up from the tip of the stirrup leather. On the off side, repeat the process so both stirrups are the same length on both sides.

If you use a rear cinch on a Western saddle, buckle it loosely. Allow about three fingers' width between the cinch and the horse's belly. It's wise to fasten the middle of the rear cinch to the front one with a connector strap.

Pick up the reins close to the saddle horn. Check the cinch a last time before you mount, sliding two or three fingers underneath the cinch or latigo. This permits the horse to breathe easily while still holding the saddle securely.

During a long ride, give your horse an occasional rest from the constant pressure of the tack. Dismount and loosen the cinch a few holes. Remind yourself about the slack cinch by hooking the near stirrup over the saddle horn.

Back at the Barn

Most riders remove the bridle, then the saddle. With the bridle replaced by the halter, you can tie the horse for unsaddling and after-ride grooming. After you dismount, bring your horse to the tying area. Locate your halter where you left it. It is often convenient to drape it over your shoulder for easy access.

Leave the reins over the horse's neck, and unbuckle the throatlatch, if equipped. With your right hand, bring the crownpiece over the ears, slowly lowering it over the forehead. When you see your horse open his mouth, continue lowering the bridle so the bit easily slips free. Avoid moving too quickly or letting the bit hit the horse's teeth.

Hold the bridle in one hand while you slip the halter in place and fasten it. Before you connect the lead rope or cross ties to the halter rings, bring the reins over the head. After you've secured the horse, hang the bridle on a nearby hook for cleaning.

You'll encounter few problems when you unsaddle your horse. Most animals appear relieved as you remove the tack, but remember to do it gently.

Reverse the saddling process, and always undo the rear cinch first. Avoid banging your horse with a swinging cinch or stirrups by laying them over the seat before you lift the saddle.

Place the saddle on a rack or on a fence rail. If you have nowhere to store it temporarily, you can prop it against a wall or post, with the pommel on the ground and the cantle resting against the wall.

Care for a sweaty back by rinsing or massaging the wet hairs. You can use a sponge or water from a hose. Wipe off excess water with a sweat scraper.

Tack Care

Before you store your tack, brush off loose hairs. You should saddle soap leather components after each use, and wash fabric pads and girths often. Also, if you notice any loosened stitching on your saddle, have it repaired as soon as possible. Brush or vacuum loose hairs from your pad. Wash it occasionally, before the fabric becomes stiff with hardened sweat.

Dip the bridle's bit into a bucket of water to wash off the metal. Store your bridle on a rounded hanger, not a nail that can crease the leather so it cracks. Let the reins hang down or loop loosely.

Because it's your primary means of control, keep your bridle in top condition. Clean leather both inside and outside, ideally after each use. Sweat, saliva, and the rubbing of metal parts can damage leather. If you notice cracks, have the bridle repaired or replace that section. Watch for wear on metal parts, too, especially the threads of Chicago screws on Western bridles. It's quite a

CURTIS MARTIN

Traditional Western attire evolved from a need for protection from the elements, livestock, and long hours in the saddle. This rider wears chinks, a form of knee-length chaps.

shock to have a screw give way so the bit falls from your horse's mouth!

Your Attire

Western riding would seem to imply cowboy gear, though you may wear any comfortable riding apparel. In competition, rules and traditions usually require distinctive Western attire. For pleasure and distance riding, choose any outfit that offers protection and comfort.

Western wear styles continue to evolve, with rodeo contestants influencing the fashions. The basic articles fulfill the function of riding wear, with two items important for safety in the saddle — boots and headgear.

A horseman always wears boots when handling livestock. A boot gives support to the foot for long hours in the saddle, and it protects the leg from chafing against the stirrup leather.

On the ground, boots protect your feet if a horse or cow steps on you. Large heels won't slide

Western Riding Attire

	Garment	Popular Varieties	Description
BASIC RIDING ATTIRE	Jeans	Wranglers	Dark blue or black Starched
	Boots	Riding boots	Stiff, high tops, scalloped, stitched for decoration Reinforced arch, high heels
		Ropers Lace-ups	
	Hat	Felt Straw	Of wool or beaver fur
	Shirt	Rodeo style	Plain cut, long sleeves, button front Brilliant colors in solids or patterns Starched
OPTIONS	Vest	Blue denim	Adds warmth
	Chaps	Shotgun Batwing Chinks Woollies	Protect legs from brush, ropes, fences Loose fitting, wrap around legs Knee length for warm weather Fur for warmth
	Bandana	Classic red	Use as a handkerchief Tie loosely around neck
	Belt	Tooled leather	Adorn with a trophy buckle or silver buckle set
		Horsehair	

This Western safety helmet meets current safety standards and is available in felt or straw styles.

Chaps protect your legs from brush, ropes, and fences.

through the stirrup, so you won't catch your foot if you or the horse falls.

The look of your boots also implies you're a horseman. Your spurs will leave gray marks on your boot heels. This mark of distinction tells the world you're "a ridin' man" (or gal).

The cowboy's traditional hat has generated controversy in today's safety-conscious society. In all equestrian disciplines *except* Western riding, horsemen recognize the value of protective headgear. When jumping, all riders wear helmets that absorb shock in case of a fall. Western riders who gallop and turn at speeds faster than most jumpers stick to their hats of felt or straw.

You can buy a felt hat with a protective shell inside. Several manufacturers offer models that meet

current safety standards. The style disguises the shell, which features a chin strap. Manufacturers report that younger riders and seniors tend to be the primary customers for this protective headwear. Unfortunately, the idea hasn't caught on with the majority of riders. Trail riders, especially distance riders, have been the only group to adopt protective headgear. In Western riding, trail riding may be the riskiest discipline, with more opportunities to fall from a moving horse.

In the Saddle: The Basics

Your body language, and that of your horse, express your equestrian skill. By your seat — the way you sit on your horse — you communicate your competence.

You don't need to look perfect. You just ride efficiently. In most Western riding, you ride for function rather than form.

Watch an expert ride. He sits firm, straight, and solid, yet relaxed and supple. He exudes confidence. His movements are fluid as he moves with the horse — just as a cowboy appears glued to the saddle.

To ride like this, you need to develop balance and timing. Through balance, your body flows with the horse as you feel his motion. Balance relates to your center of gravity, just like the horse's balance. Instructor Sue Cummins has used the term *centering* to describe that balance: "It's where all the energy and the flow comes from."

She has described the centered rider as authentic. With a genuine balance, you sit in the saddle

A balanced rider sits softly on the horse, riding with the motion.

with your legs falling down relaxed over the horse. Your arms hang down softly, also relaxed, and your vision is straight ahead.

Riding resembles other sports, in which the athlete moves from a base without rigidity. If you pose, hold your breath, move from your shoulder or chin, or stare, the tension makes you look and feel tight and rigid rather than relaxed and elastic.

Your horse feels your body language. You communicate your tension to him, often without realizing it. Cummins has cautioned against concentrating too much on sitting "correctly." "When you ride stiffly 'in position,' your horse doesn't like it. The horse wants to feel a softness on him. He wants to feel a flow. He wants to feel a partnership."

Learning balance and timing does demand a focus. Before you can experience that fluid feeling on horseback, you need to develop physical skills.

Mounting Up

With your horse ready to ride, check your tack one final time. Lead your horse by the reins to a clear, level area. You'll usually mount on the left (near) side, although the Western horse should be trained for you to mount from either side.

Make sure that the horse stands quietly and balanced on all four legs. While you mount, he must stand still. You're in a precarious position between the ground and the saddle, and a sudden movement could cause you to fall. Maintain control by keeping a hand on the reins at all times.

Stand with your left shoulder beside the horse's neck, and place the reins over the horse's head so they rest on the withers. With separate (split) reins, you can drape the near rein to the off side, and the off-side rein to the near side. Shorten them just enough so you have control.

With your left hand, hold onto the reins and a fistful of the mane. You can mount facing the saddle or slightly toward the rear so you're looking over the horse's offside hip. Facing the saddle, you can watch to make sure he doesn't move, and use your right hand to twist the stirrup toward you. Place your left foot in the stirrup and hop up with your right foot.

As you push off the ground, shift your rein hand from the mane to the saddle horn. Swing your right leg over the saddle and gently settle yourself in the seat. Place your right foot in the right stirrup.

Aim for a continuous, smooth movement. Try to alight into the saddle; do not plop down with all your weight.

If you suspect that the horse might move while you mount, maintain a lateral flexion with the reins. Shorten the near side rein so the horse bends his neck toward you, and say, "Whoa."

To dismount, you reverse the steps. Remove your right foot from the stirrup. Stand up and turn toward the horse's off-side hip to swing your right leg behind you. As you move toward the ground, keep your left foot in the stirrup. Remove it as your right heel touches the ground, and step down.

During the dismount, keep the reins on the horse's neck so you maintain control. You should face forward, standing beside your horse's neck, to complete the movement.

When mounting, aim for a continuous, smooth movement, and ease gently into the saddle.

Sitting Correctly

Your seat is where you gain security and softness, blending the two sensations for a graceful posture. Sit in a comfortable, natural way, in the middle of the horse.

You should look as comfortable as you feel. Sitting from your center, you sit vertically — an imaginary line from your ear down through your shoulder and hip would touch the back of your heel. Hold your back straight and flat, yet not arched so you look stiff.

Imagine that the horse has disappeared, and you are standing on the ground, and maintain that same posture in the saddle.

California trainer Mack Linn has taught: "Riding a horse is just like standing here. Stand up and sit straight down without being stiff. Stand up, drop back, and keep that position. You bend only at the knee and hip." He advises that to loosen up, you can stand up, turn right and sit, then stand up and turn left and sit.

With an ideal stirrup length, your knee is bent slightly so your heel is lower than your toe. Your legs hang down at or slightly behind the cinch. If you feel as if you're reaching for the stirrups, or your knees are bent too much, test the length by standing up so your weight is off the horse's back. You shouldn't have more than an inch or two between your crotch and the seat of the saddle. If more or less than that, dismount and adjust the length on both sides.

Place your foot in the stirrup so your weight rests on the widest part of your foot. Flex your ankles to absorb the shock, but don't press hard on the stirrups. Pushing will tense your body and brace your legs so they move to the sides, away from the horse. You should be able to feel the warmth of contact with him, along your thighs, knees, and upper calf.

In this balanced position, you can move with the horse, yet remain steady. You effectively control him with your body weight, hands, and legs. You feel close to him, and you can meld with his movements.

Hold the reins in one hand, your left. (If you're left-handed, switch to holding reins in your right

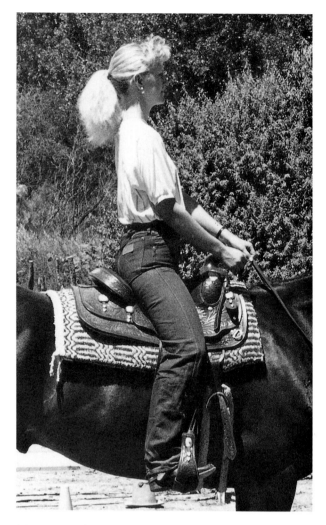

To sit correctly, imagine a line from your ear down through your shoulder and hip to the back of your heel.

hand.) Adopted from the working cowboy, this style leaves your dominant hand free to open a gate, swing a rope, or crack a whip.

You can hold the reins in a fist, with the lines coming up through your fist. Or, hold your first finger (or two fingers) between the reins. Whichever style, most trainers advise to keep your thumb up and knuckles facing forward. This gives you effective control and an "elastic" hand.

Hold your rein hand slightly in front of the saddle horn so it's parallel to the ground, in line with the horse's neck. Try to keep your hand in that spot, slightly ahead of your hip. You can rest your free hand on your thigh, let it hang by your side, or hold it at waist level.

You sit in the center of the saddle, and you feel the horse through your seat bones. You also have contact through your legs and hands.

Maintain a guiding contact, not too tense or too passive. Hold the reins so that with only a light movement, you contact the horse's mouth.

Hold your rein hand steady, but not completely rigid. Don't worry about keeping your elbows in, or you'll tense the joint. Let the joint relax and go with the horse, absorbing the shock.

Learn to sit down, so you won't move and pull on the horse's mouth. You maintain the vertical position at all three gaits. You move slightly back and forth with the horse's motion, and you appear fluid and supple.

Reining

You guide the horse in the saddle as you do on the ground. Your body language cues the horse to respond.

The light touch of the neck rein cues the horse to turn.

In addition to your rein, cue your horse with your weight. Shift to the right to signal a bend. Both horses in these photos are "between the reins."

"A cue is a signal between you and your horse," trainer John Lyons has said. "You set up the condition often enough so you get the correct response to happen. If you don't get your response, go to a point where you set it up and repeat, repeat, repeat, until the response becomes automatic."

For the signals, you use the aids of hands, legs, body weight, and seat bones. Every horseman aims for good hands, a give and take. When you apply a cue, the horse answers and you instantly stop the cue. Although you work on a loose rein, at times you'll ride on contact. You maintain a sensitive feel of the horse's mouth and keep the horse "between the reins."

You'll spend many hours in the saddle learning the right amount of feel. On contact, your hand will move with the motion of the horse's neck. You'll gently let your hand go forward and back at the walk, to keep the pressure consistent. Don't hold your hand rigid, so the reins alternate between taut and slack. If you pull on the reins as the horse moves forward, you're clashing your aids.

The Western horse turns with the neck rein, turning away from the feel of a rein laid on his neck. If you want to turn right, first you look to the right. Keep your hand low, but move it to the right to lay the rein on the left side of the neck.

Try to move your hand only as far as the distance over your saddle swells. Any further, and you'll start "cranking" the horse's neck with the opposite rein. The horse might tilt his head to the outside, instead of bending in the direction of travel. You want him to follow his nose as he walks forward in an arc.

Trainers consider the neck rein an indirect rein. A direct rein is a direct pull, toward the direction you want to go. (Western riders often call this the "plow rein.") Texas educator Terry McCutcheon has taught students to understand the concept of the indirect rein.

"So many riders tend to pull across the neck, which gets the horse's nose turned to the outside. We teach how the horse moves in one direction with the direct rein, his head and neck in position. Then you use the indirect rein to follow that, and use the leg to push the horse in the direction set by the rein. You need to understand the combination of a leg and the indirect rein."

Lay the rein, release the pressure, and lay it again on the neck. The horse should move his neck and body to turn the corner. If he doesn't, squeeze your outside leg (the leg on the side away from the direction you're turning) against the horse. This reinforces your rein cue. Squeeze and release.

Halting

The understanding that develops between you and your horse begins with "Whoa." You know that when you give the command, the horse willingly obeys. Your horsemanship depends on this mutual understanding: "Whoa" means stop right now.

Use your voice first, and easily take up the rein. This cue relies on pressure and reward, just as in handling the horse on the ground. You give, or release pressure, to reward him for a correct response.

Ideally, he responds to the halt cue because he wants to please you, not because you have forced him. He's learned the path of least resistance, which is to submit his will to yours. He also anticipates that you will respond by rewarding him with lack of pressure.

The correct leg position will help keep you steady and secure. With your heels dropped, hold your calves against the horse's barrel. Your feet should point forward or slightly out.

Both of you gain mutual confidence through this simple response. The two of you read each other. The way your horse halts tells you how he's feeling — willing or resistant. The way you apply and release pressure tells him what kind of rider you are. You're working with your horse so he performs, regardless of what he wants. You'll expand that feeling at each gait, and then develop the comfort and relaxation of a secure partnership.

Walking

Nudge the horse to walk. Either touch him with your heels, or squeeze with your calves. As he moves, you absorb his motion and remain one with him. Keep your shoulders square and your head up.

To gain that authentic seat, don't force your body into a posed position. Texas trainer Nancy Cahill has advised learning by sitting on the horse and feeling your own balance. "Just go ride, without someone saying 'Do this, do that,'" she says. "Ride in a safe place. Ride smart and don't abuse the horse, and it's okay if you bounce. You'll find how to sit in the middle some day, to sit in the middle and find your balance."

Sit down in the saddle on your seat bones, and think of the seat as your spine. With an ideal seat, your spine fuses with the horse's spine. You feel the support of the horse's hind legs with your seat. There's a feeling of togetherness, with no gap between you.

When you relax, you feel what the horse is doing. His back ripples as he moves in the four-beat walk, and he swings his neck up, down, and sideways. With a loose rein, he swings the neck in rhythm with the legs.

Learn to feel the horse, so you can respond to his movements. Trainer Terry Berg has advised: "You're going to feel it before you see it, or feel it in your hands when he starts to slow down, or he starts to speed up."

While holding your body vertical, start absorbing in your foundation, your feet. Pull your legs back under you, breaking at the ankle and lifting the toe so you drop your heel.

Instructor John Richard Young has coached riders to keep their seat steady, using their legs while releasing the rein: "Control your legs in order to control the horse."

With your heels dropped, you'll find it natural to hold your calves against the horse's barrel. This position will help keep you steady and secure and your legs quiet. Feel the insides of your calves against the horse, with the upper part of your boots touching his sides. Your feet point forward or slightly out.

Your knees point forward, without grabbing. Grabbing establishes a pivot point. Your lower leg will tend to swing back and forth instead of remaining quiet. You can maintain contact with your entire leg, keeping it "open."

If you push too much weight against the stirrups, you push your crotch out of the saddle. Let your weight settle in your seat. Sitting still helps your horse move smoothly.

You might find that you slouch, propping your buttocks against the cantle. You lose that vertical line, so aim to remain forward rather than back. Your torso remains in line with your leg and hip.

California trainer Dave Rhodes has said: "Remember to keep your feet still and quiet, and keep the top half of the body still and quiet. Let the hips move with the horse's motion. Don't get to rocking with the motion like you're riding down the trail on a Saturday afternoon."

Look where you're going, with your eyes up so you look between the horse's ears. Looking down can cause you to lean forward, out of balance.

Jogging

Moving from the walk to the halt involves a transition. To move out of the walk, you practice upward transitions into faster gaits like the jog or lope. Downward transitions occur from the jog to the walk, or the lope to the jog.

Achieve transitions through your voice, hands, legs, and seat bones. Keep your back strong when you change gait, to absorb the shift in movement.

Coordinating aids takes practice. You want to use your "gas" to push the horse forward with

To absorb the jogging motion, relax and let your hips go with the horse.

energy, yet you channel that energy with aids that "brake" and guide the horse.

Coordinate your balance with your timing. "Timing is to get the horse to respond and to make the corrections at the right time," Arabian horse trainer Jim Porcher has said. "Balance is the confidence to know that you're there and will take charge of the horse. You have that kind of balance so you don't act after the fact."

Allow the horse to go forward. Integrate your cues so you don't confuse him. Keep your arm and fingers elastic on the reins, so you don't pull back while urging him forward.

For this simple acceleration of gait, check your balance. Drop your legs back and under you. Depending on how your horse is trained, nudge with the inside leg or both legs and cluck (click your tongue) to ask for the jog. Make your cue subtle, yet definite.

The horse jogs in a two-beat gait, which varies in roughness from horse to horse. Some are

smooth, so you can easily sit with minimal motion, your seat glued to the saddle. You'll move with the horse. Other horses move roughly, jostling you back and forth at each step.

To absorb the motion, relax and let your hips go with the horse. Your upper body remains relaxed and quiet. Dave Rhodes has suggested that you concentrate on the bouncing up and down. "Not to post, but to go up and down with the motion. When I judge riders and see them coming down the rail, I see a lot less motion on the up and down rider than when I watch one who goes back and forth."

This is a conscious movement that counteracts the movement that's already happening. Rhodes suggests that you tap your feet on the stirrups, because that foot movement will work against the horse's motion. Tapping helps your feet become still, and you absorb the motion.

Jim Porcher has offered a different suggestion. "Take the shock in your hips, sideways — left hip, right hip. Your upper body shouldn't bounce more than your horse's topline. If you tighten up, you start to bounce."

Learn the rhythm of the jog, and concentrate on maintaining it. Your horse may try to escape you by speeding up to a trot or slowing down to a walk or halt. If he trots fast, don't lean forward or pinch with your knees. Stand up in the stirrups if you feel yourself wobbling, with your body vertical or slightly behind the vertical.

To move down to the walk, sit tall, say "Whoa," and apply rein pressure. Release the reins as soon as he slows.

Don't let your horse "die" into a downward transition before you have given the cue. If you feel him start dragging, squeeze him lightly with your heels and release. You might also make a clucking noise.

With practice, you'll keep your legs steady as the horse jogs. You'll learn to ride the gait's diagonal motion with your body, absorbing in a fluid manner that's somewhere between rigid and rubbery. Your joints — ankles, knees, hips — should feel strong yet elastic.

Loping

When you want to lope to the left, bend the horse's nose slightly to the inside. This moves the hindquarter to the left, which affects the lead he'll take.

You'll use your outside leg, in this case your right leg, to tell the horse to lope. Keep him slightly bent in the direction of the lead you want him to lope on. Trainers call these "diagonal aids," when you combine aids on two sides of the horse.

Your horse may only respond to more basic lateral aids, where you apply both rein and leg aids on the same side. Here you'd bend the head to the outside when you press with the outside leg.

You'll feel your horse thrust forward as he strikes the lope. Keep your body back. Pull your shoulders away from your hands to sit tall. Your back should feel strong in this upward transition, and your seat should remain square, with weight in your heels. Avoid rocking forward into the lope.

Sit the lope. If your horse lopes smoothly, without rolling or rocking his back, you can easily keep your seat so only your pelvis, seat, and thighs stretch forward with each stride. On a rougher horse, you may feel that your buttocks pound against the saddle at every stride.

You want the motion to flow down into your heels. Dave Rhodes has suggested that you try standing in the stirrups and pushing your hips forward, while holding onto the saddle horn. "Push with the lower part of your back. Push from the back of the saddle to the front. You do it in time with the horse's movements."

Once you learn this pushing movement, you can slide lightly back into the saddle and absorb the circular, longeing motion. You let your hips go along with the horse's back, and the horse accepts the weight of your seat.

"The top half of your body will stay still and quiet, and your feet will stay still and quiet. You'll have that good base of support, and you'll be right up with the motion of your horse," explains Rhodes.

Learn to follow the up and down motion, as the horse seems to rise and fall. Florida trainer

At the lope, you should be sitting tall with your seat square and weight in your heels.

To lope to the left, apply the left (inside) rein and your right (outside) leg. The use of aids on both sides of the horse is called "diagonal aids."

An alternate method, which uses more basic "lateral aids," is to apply the right (outside) rein and your right (outside) leg.

Andy Moorman has used the image of a Ferris wheel to explain the movement. "Understand what the gait does, what legs are doing what, and that the horse will come up and come back down. You don't fall forward or back. You just stay right in the middle. As the horse comes down, keep your legs in place so the horse comes back up again."

Nancy Cahill has explained that you need to feel the full stride of the lope. "I count a full stride, one, two, three. Don't count *one*-two-three, *one*-two-three, or it's a 'Lawrence Welk' waltzing feel. Get into the cadence and rhythm with your body."

Your horse should not gain speed in the lope. If he does move out more quickly than you want, open the angle of your upper body to a position slightly behind the vertical. This tells him, "Wait for me," while you "bump" him with the reins.

From the lope, you perform a downward transition to the jog, and then to the walk. Use your voice to say "Whoa" (or whatever word your horse responds to) and sink into the saddle for the change in gait. Make your lower leg grow longer with weight in your

heels. Raise your toes up to absorb the changed movement. Don't press down with your toes, because you'll push yourself up out of the saddle.

Learning Your Leads

Four-footed animals lope (canter or gallop) in the same way, in a three-beat gait with a period of suspension. They lope with front and rear legs on the same side moving in unison.

When a horse lopes on the left lead, he moves his left hind and left front legs forward in a sweeping motion. The left front and left hind feet hit the ground a moment before and further forward than the right feet.

On the right lead, the right feet strike the ground ahead of the left ones. The horse chooses which lead to take, depending on the direction of travel.

You direct your horse to take the correct lead. You maintain the animal's balance by selecting the side you will turn. If you are circling a pen in a clockwise direction, you should cue for the right lead.

On the right lead, the right front and hind feet "lead" the left and hit the ground before the left feet.

At the lope on the left lead, the left front and hind feet hit the ground (or "lead") a moment before and ahead of the right feet.

If a horse is on the wrong lead for the direction he's bending, he'll have to work harder to maintain his balance. He might shift into what's called "cross-firing," or a disunited lope, such as leading with the left front and right hind. If he does this, you'd feel a rough, bumping motion, not the smooth rocking of the correct lope. Stop your horse immediately and cue him to lope again.

Whenever you signal your horse to lope, check to make sure he started in the correct lead. At first, you'll have to look at his shoulders to be able to tell which lead he took. If you're loping to the right, his right shoulder should extend slightly farther forward than the left. On a horse that takes long strides, you can see his hoof reaching forward.

Don't lean far forward to check, which compromises your balance and might bother the horse.

Humane Riding

Pay attention to how your horse feels when you ride. When you first start on a ride, let him relax at a slow walk on a loose rein. Don't make him go to work right away, but allow his body and mind to warm up.

Listen to his body language while you're in the saddle. An alert animal should feel businesslike and purposeful. He moves forward confidently, yet he listens to your aids.

Blend compassion with authority. Know what your horse can do, and don't ask him to perform the impossible.

If you feel his gait become uneven, stop and dismount to check his feet. He may have stepped on a rock, or injured a part of his leg.

Recognize boredom and fatigue. Don't always ride the same way in the same place, and avoid wearing out your horse. If he seems too slow, shortens his stride, or stumbles, he may be tired. Slow down, or stop and rest for a moment. A tired horse can hurt himself, or even stumble and fall.

Learn to glance down to determine the lead, and continue riding. Eventually you'll learn to sense by feel, and you can tell the moment your horse strides correctly into either lead.

Galloping

The gallop is a faster lope, usually not an all-out run. (You should only run a horse on a racetrack.) Ride only as fast as you feel comfortable. Don't gallop to see how fast he can run; the all-out speed can turn your horse into an uncontrollable runaway.

With a balanced seat at all gaits, you refine your position. You can adapt to a specialty sport that requires a more forward posture, such as reining.

Keeping Your Balance

Whatever discipline you follow, you move with the horse, with a straight posture. You stabilize your seat so there is no excess motion or wobbling, yet you feel strong and elastic, not rigid.

Overcome any natural tendencies, mainly leaning in the wrong direction. This affects the horse's performance, as well as puts you in a precarious position.

Trainers agree that the novice rider focuses on a fear of falling. In fact, if you distill the essence of equitation, it's to keep your balance so you don't fall off.

"Riding a horse can be a very frightening experience," Terry McCutcheon has said. "Beginners will literally throw away the reins when they grab the horn. That scares them, because no matter how hard they pull or push, sometimes they can't gain control."

Counteract the leaning by keeping your shoulders square, pulling them back. If you start to lean forward, reach back and pat the horse on the rear. This also steadies your seat.

Never use your hands to control your balance. Your arms and hands must operate independently of your seat. A hand that flaps or bounces — or a tense, gripping hand that fights the horse's move-

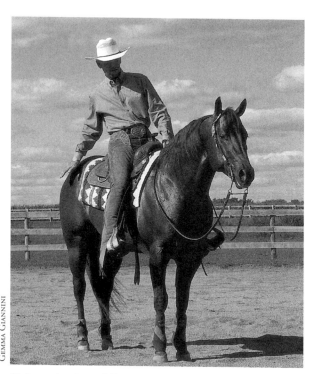

Balance in the saddle is important. If you tend to lean forward, take a moment now and then to reach back and pat the horse on the rear.

Keep a light touch on the reins. Never use a tense or gripping fist — this will only fight your horse's movements. Your free hand can rest lightly on your thigh.

Safety in the Saddle

Riding is a risky sport, and riders do fall off. You can prevent this common accident by developing a secure, balanced seat.

Ride in a ring, under supervision, until you feel your horse responds obediently to you. Learn how to fall safely by practicing vaulting off at a walk. You should be able to swing your right leg over the back and slide to the ground, away from the horse.

An accident can occur at any time, so don't let your attention wander. As you adjust tack or your riding gear, maintain control over the horse. Never drop the reins to adjust your spur; loop your arm through the reins to retain control.

Riding past a frightening distraction tests your safe riding skills. If your horse is afraid, you'll feel his heart pounding under your legs. Here you must project a feeling of confidence, to override the horse's fear. Demand that he focus on you, not the fearful stimulus.

Keep your heels down in the stirrups. This posi-tion strengthens your foundation and also allows you to slide your feet out of the stirrups if you do lose your balance and start to fall.

Any horse might slip, even when walking. Allow him to have his head if you feel him stumble or lose his footing. If he does fall, slide off on the side toward which he's falling. You'll land away from his legs, avoiding a kick as he thrashes.

Practice safety in the arena, around other riders. Wait to enter the ring until no one's near the gate. Quickly move into the arena's center, so you don't obstruct riders on the rail. Walk your horse on the inside track, allowing faster riders the rail, and halt in the center. If you pass riders going in the same direction, call "Passing" as you pass them on the inside. Stay to your right if you pass in the opposite direction.

Always maintain one horse's length — 8 feet minimum — between your horse and others. Never let your horse bite or kick another animal, and watch out for neighboring horses yourself.

ment — demonstrates poor horsemanship and lack of control.

As you ride, continually check your position and adjust yourself. By maintaining your seat, you'll improve your equitation. Adjust your seat or hands when you discover they've moved.

If you feel your saddle veering right or left, you can use your weight to shift it back to the middle of the horse's back. On the "low" side, grip slightly with your knee and hitch the weight of your hip and leg to move the saddle over.

Also check your rein length, your position in the saddle, and your feet in the stirrups. Review your body angle and foot position before and after a transition to another gait, and at set locations around your riding area. By adjusting your position, you establish the habits of an effective rider. Both you and the horse stay comfortable.

Feeling the Rhythm

As the horse moves through his three gaits, your body moves softly in rhythm to the footfalls. You instinctively develop a sense of timing.

"You as a rider are an integral part of that balance and rhythm of the horse," Andy Moorman has explained. "If you cause the balance to go away, or the rhythm, then you lose the feel. If the horse starts to lose his rhythm, you have to be able to enhance it."

Moorman advises counting with the horse's strides. This helps you to relax down on the horse's back and to feel his rhythm. She says: "That's when you know that a person is starting to be a rider, when she begins to exhibit the feel of knowing where she is, and where the horse is. It's a language. You have to speak to the horse in a language he understands."

You also protect the horse's rhythm. If you feel him "stutter" at the lope or jog, or begin to lose his forward energy, squeeze with your legs for a moment.

Your mind can affect the horse's rhythm. Many trainers use visualization. Trainer Pat Parelli has described this as "having a clear picture in your mind, then getting that picture to go through your body to your horse." Horses sense your thoughts even if you simply imagine slowing down or speeding up.

"Horses are smart by how they feel, not smart in the sense of scientific intelligence tests," Terry Berg has said. "They are extremely sensitive. Even the dullest horses are much more sensitive than people realize."

Maintaining Control

Most horses want to please their riders. They respond to seek comfort.

For the horse, comfort may mean he's in charge. As the horseman, you need to radiate the sense of authority. You're riding the horse — the horse isn't riding you!

In your handling, seek a balance between firm and gentle. You want to keep the horse soft and responsive, submissive and obedient. In return, he learns to trust you.

You exert authority, just as you do on the ground. Yet, you must keep your seat to maintain your control.

Terry Berg described how a rider can easily let her horse have "the upper hoof." "If the horse starts to do something, you lean forward. That's probably the worst place to be at that particular time, because then you've let the horse have his own decision, as opposed to thinking about your decision."

Because of the horse's attention span, you must resolve each action immediately. Don't realize a moment later that your horse ignored you.

Even a trained horse can evade your command and need a reprimand. You answer by correcting the horse, then rewarding him with a loose rein. You leave him alone when he's correct. He learns that a free rein rewards him, and when you pick up the reins, you'll maintain your aids until he performs to your standards.

Give and take relates to pressure and reward. When you have to take up the rein or use your leg, you follow up by giving, or removing the pressure.

You must recognize when your horse responds. "If you question yourself whether the horse responded or he didn't, then he probably didn't," Berg has said. "It's a yes or no situation, and you ride with that definite feeling. You have to follow through, to answer."

The horse may duck his head, or "root," to gain a looser rein. Don't "jerk his face," but react with a fixed hand. When you feel a stiffness, close your fingers on the reins and brace your back, or make your back less flexible. You don't let him dictate to you to soften — you wait for him to accept your hand and stop pulling.

You may need to "bump" your horse. Tighten contact for a moment, then release to reward. Don't take hold and irritate the horse.

Gary Ferguson, a California Arabian trainer, has noted that riders have trouble with balancing control and softness. "You need to understand that when you use pressure, you get pressure back. The first thing riders do is grab and not relax."

Control means command of the hindquarters. The horse moves his feet through impulsion from his hindquarters.

Your horse must go forward at your command. John Richard Young has said: "When you squeeze with your legs, he should instantly take off. A horse needs impulsion, and a horse that has impulsion is a free goer. He doesn't pull, but he goes freely. You can't work a horse if he won't go forward. Your horse will be behind the bit and only go backwards. You can't do anything."

Get the horse to focus on his job — to move you forward. He goes in the direction you want with minimal cues from you. You shouldn't have to move your upper body or exert yourself, because the horse should respond to your leg aids.

This horse is working toward collection, based on the rider's insisting leg aid.

How an Instructor Can Help

An instructor can coach you and help you form good habits through precise explanations and timely suggestions. A good teacher allows you to gain confidence. He challenges you to polish your abilities and to learn new skills, but he keeps you in a safety zone so you don't get physically scared.

Can anyone learn to be a competent rider? Most instructors say yes. Nancy Cahill has compared riding to playing the piano. "There are natural talents, and there are those who have to work harder than the average person. All you have to do is want to, because desire can overcome."

The person who helped you find your horse might be an instructor. Or, you might take riding

Riding Bareback

Some instructors feel that riding bareback, without a saddle, helps you develop a stable seat. Without the pommel, cantle, or stirrups to hold you, you gain an exceptional sense of balance through your entire body. Balance is what keeps you on the horse.

"We start our students bareback," explains Terry McCutcheon. "So they don't have to worry about control, a partner leads the horse. We ask the rider to feel where those feet are, and what part of her leg is most depending or working the most at any particular time, going one direction or another. Knowing where those feet are supposed to be, you start to understand the horse better and become more confident.

"We're trying to develop a muscle memory. Instead of relying on the saddle horn, you kick in a particular part of the body to help you adjust to whatever comes up."

You'll also learn to feel every step the horse takes. To become a true partner, you must understand the sequence of footfalls in the three gaits. You'll move closer to him, and you'll be able to influence him more subtly as his body language communicates with you.

Bareback, your seat feels the forward strides that begin in the hindquarters. All horses move their four legs, but the action begins in the powerful muscles that propel the hind legs forward.

When a horse walks, trots, or lopes, he first moves a hind foot forward. You may not be able to see this from the ground, but riding bareback, you can feel the shifting of weight begin behind your seat.

To mount, either use a mounting block or position your horse beside a fence. You can also mount by springing across his back, if he'll stand. Try to jump so your upper body rests over the horse, and then straighten up.

Sit with your center of balance over the horse's center of balance. You should maintain a vertical posture, and avoid letting your body angle ahead or behind the vertical.

As the horse moves, you move with him.

You're not right over his withers, but slightly back so you feel the motion of the hindquarters close behind you. Don't move your body and expect the horse to catch up with you.

The first time you ride bareback, you'll feel tense and insecure. Resist the urge to grab with your knees or heels. Gripping won't keep you in place, and the movement can excite the horse and start a chain reaction. He speeds up, you grab tighter, and you lose your sense of balance while pulling back on the reins.

Absorb the horse's motion through your thighs. Drape your legs so you contact the horse lightly with your calves, and keep your heels out of his sides until you need to cue him to move or turn.

Riding bareback can give you a poise and confidence you may never experience otherwise. You can truly share the sensation of two beings moving in unison.

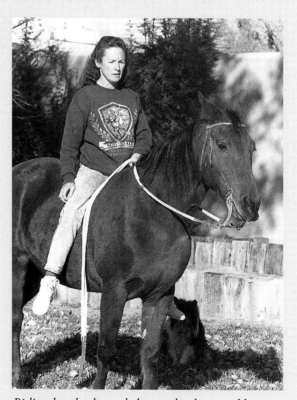

Riding bareback can help you develop a stable seat.

lessons from a person who specializes in your type of riding. You can also attend riding clinics, hosted by local or visiting professionals.

A sympathetic teacher has to adjust to your learning style. He should inspire you through basic methods of explanation, demonstration, and instruction. He should articulate what he expects.

Instructors find different ways of explaining physical sensations. Many use visual imagery and analogies to illustrate what you should feel. Andy Moorman has found that a novice can watch and imitate a good demonstration rider. "I point out to students exactly what's happening all the while, and they really see it. A lot of times it's just seeing what the person doesn't do. 'See how still she is?'"

Cahill has said: "You learn a timing and feel that don't come into words. When you get close, I say, 'Did you feel that? That's what you want to feel. Whatever you felt then, that's what looked the best.' I can hardly get those words out of my mouth fast enough, and it's gone."

Make the most of lessons by respecting your teacher's advice. Listen closely and trust him or her, and try to respond honestly.

Moorman has challenged pessimistic riders who fear trying a new exercise. "They find out they really can do something. When they quit worrying about not being able to do it, they start figuring out *how* to do it. The only reason you can't do it is you don't think you can. Think in the positive, not the negative."

When you're a beginner, your teacher should walk you through the basics and move you through phases. He should patiently support you through positive feedback.

A teacher breaks down riding skills into fundamental steps. Your instructor might put you on a longe line to help you relax your stiffness and acquire a secure seat. This is an accepted method, often used by instructors throughout the world. You learn to refine your balance, without having to worry about controlling the horse's speed, straightness, or rhythm at the same time.

Appaloosa trainer Alpha Russell starts all students on the longe line. "You learn to balance at all gaits with no reins. You see if your body's twisted, or your leg is weak. Your body is trained so you won't support yourself with the reins. You can focus completely on your leg or shoulder, so you're a safe rider."

When you get to a certain level of skill, you reach a plateau where you begin to act instinctively. You can feel the horse's responses and distinguish correct from incorrect. You don't need a person telling you every step. A teacher can step back and suggest what to do, and then let you experiment. You find solutions within yourself. Thinking on your own, you feel the horse and figure out your next move.

You can also learn through group lessons. Here you ride with one or more riders at your same level of expertise. Observe the others, and listen to what your instructor tells them.

Your Horse, Your Teacher

Master horsemen agree that the horse is the ultimate teacher. Even the equestrian with decades of experience continues to learn from each animal's unique responses.

Like people, horses share similarities and individual differences. The more horses you ride, the more you'll learn about equine behaviors.

An instructor should have you work with horses that will teach you. Terry McCutcheon has explained how he builds a rider's confidence by matching him or her with a horse: "We put the most experienced horses with the least experienced people. The horse's level of performance will gravitate toward the rider's ability. Especially old school horses will do as little as possible, but as much as they're asked. The intermediate or advanced rider has the horse with the least experience, so she has to look for a particular result."

Becoming a
Western Rider

With practice, any rider can become a horseman. As you develop physical balance and coordination, you can also learn how to influence the horse to achieve a superior performance.

You are the dominant partner, but you don't control the horse by brute force. You lead him, just as you do on the ground, by maintaining mutual respect. When he's amenable to your commands and willingly performs as you expect, you leave him alone to concentrate on his job.

When you are working with your horse, you seek finesse. In the saddle, your timing will be crucial, because you must sense when and how much to apply your aids.

When you're patient and take your time, you'll gain a closer partnership. The two of you agree on a subtle yet powerful communication. You feel him being light and loose, not scared or resistant. You let him show his athleticism and style, moving with energy and brilliance.

Teaching the Horse

Although you don't claim the title of horse trainer, you teach your horse every time you ride him. You set up specific conditions, and he responds. Your reactions to his responses train him.

Whenever you handle or ride your horse, you're always teaching him a good or a bad habit. You want to instill and reinforce good habits, for steady and consistent movements. You can achieve this through reprimands. When he makes a mistake, you correct him. You consistently repeat the correction, and these reactions direct him to improve what he's doing. Training the horse relies on the animal's motivation. He responds to you primarily to avoid pain.

Trainer Terry Berg has used the word *finished* to describe the broke horse. "Can you easily rein him? Will he stop and turn around easily? Will he lope off when you kiss to him and squeeze?"

She added that most horses aren't finished, or trained, to this level of partnership. Whatever the level of your horse, you need to determine what responses you want from him in every situation. He learns to work for you, to surrender to your request. He knows that if he doesn't submit, you'll repeat your cue and even get after him.

Berg has stressed that when you pick up a rein, you don't release the rein cue until your horse responds. You know what you want to communicate, you move your hand or fingers, and you concentrate on that reply to your request. She explained: "If you pick your horse up and put some pressure on the reins, at that point in time you need to make an automatic decision. The horse tells you something. If he's real soft and gives to you, that's probably the end of it. Whatever you asked for has occurred. But if he leans on you, and you haven't responded to him, he's told you something. You've lost authority right at that point in time."

Establish credibility with your horse. For every action, you expect a reaction. You don't ignore his action, because he'll learn a bad habit. When you act with authority, the horse knows that you mean what you say.

"Learning to ride is learning to be quietly assertive," trainer Gill Swarbrick has said. "The inner confidence has to come from you. If you're a person who has respect for yourself and your capabilities in other areas, you won't lack confidence."

Because the horse is sensitive, don't confuse him with constant signals. "Picking" at him, or fiddling with the reins or repeated jabs with your heels, can make him "dead" to the aids. Assert yourself with a decisive, definite command, and repeat the signal more strongly if necessary.

The definite command doesn't need to be harsh. Use as light a pressure as your horse recognizes, as most horses respect their riders and want to avoid a reprimand. He's learned that if he responds to the light signal, he avoids the heavier one that you'd apply. He stays comfortable, you leave him alone, and he's less likely to rebel.

Vary the intensity to teach and test responses. Trainer Casey Hinton has advised: "Start out

Use as light a pressure on the reins as the horse will recognize. As he learns to respond to a light signal, he will avoid the heavier ones.

with five pounds of pressure. When the horse limbers up, go down to two pounds." Or if you have to intensify the amount, the reprimand teaches the horse to react with the maneuver you've requested. He learns not to make the mistake again.

Hinton has noted that you can make your horse better by allowing him to make a mistake, and fine-tuning the response. He calls this, "Daring your horse to fail to respond. If you ask with less, you can reprimand, and your horse gets lighter as he starts to read your mind. You want him to wonder what you're going to do next, and to wait for you."

The amount of pressure you apply to the horse should fit the situation. A good trainer is firm and consistent and gets to know the horse's limitations. This rider applies cues to help the mare move in balance. The horse bends slightly to the inside in response to his outside leg and rein. The mare lopes smoothly and "on the bit." She reaches well underneath herself with the inside hind leg.

The amount of pressure should fit the situation. Trainer Pat Parelli has called this a "just" attitude. "You cause responses, and you don't force or plead. If you have to get firm, you do it without getting mean or mad. You trust your horse to respond, and you're ready to correct. It's not more of one than the other."

A good teacher is firm, consistent, and understanding. A good horse trainer learns the horse's limitations. He doesn't force or abuse the animal to make it perform movements beyond its ability. A horseman lets the horse know when it's done well. The horse acquires the trainer's disposition, so a steady trainer produces a steady horse.

For you to communicate with your horse, practice the communication system he knows. Find out how much of a cue you need, and how sensitive he is. Aim for subtle signals, starting by visualizing what you want him to do. Follow up your expectation with a physical cue. If he resists or doesn't respond, assert your request by repeating the cue, and then increase the strength of your signal.

You teach him to be lighter and more perceptive, so he feels soft and relaxed. Terry Berg has explained: "When you're on a good horse, it's like you think the movement and it occurs. To me, that is the ultimate. And it's fun!"

Listen to Your Horse

In the saddle, you can anticipate your horse's behavior by tuning into his body language. Watch his ears, because he points his ears where he looks. Does he signal what he's thinking before he acts?

Your aids tell him to gather himself for a change in direction or gait, or to move on with more impulsion or speed. Test your horse's responses to you. Lean forward and back to see if he'll speed up or slow down. Reach down to touch your toe, or back to tap the croup. Move into a jog on a loose rein, and think about the halt. Does the horse tune into your thought and slow down on his own? Ask for the halt, and see if he responds quickly or seems to ignore or evade your aids.

You can also feel what a horse is thinking, and you can learn to feel how he expresses anxiety. An-

Trotting is the easiest gait for the horse and an excellent warm up exercise.

ticipate any behavior, and ride assertively. Horses tend to repeat their reactions, so you can correct incidents of shying, rearing, or bucking before the misbehavior occurs.

He may test you by evading or resisting. Know how much to press, and when to back off. Here you maintain your self-control, because you don't want to start a fight. While you don't want to submit to

his behavior, you do want to preserve his respect.

You can break the cycle of misbehavior through channeling the horse's energies into work. Your basic goal in riding is forward motion, cueing the horse to move forward.

When in doubt, go forward. In motion, you've gotten the horse's attention and he's submitted to your will. For example, instead of making a nervous beast stand still, put him into a long trot (an extended jog) to take the edge off. This gets his muscles moving freely.

Pat Parelli has emphasized the trot as an excellent exercise: "Let him trot on a loose rein until you get rid of that impulsiveness. Turn the impulsiveness into impulsion. The trot is the easiest gait for the horse, the middle of the road — not as slow and boring as the walk, and not as fatiguing as the canter."

Terry Berg adds advice about using the trot, noting that some riders make the mistake of trying to jog first. "Warm up at a posting trot. When your horse is ready to think about jogging, put his head and neck and body in frame [rounded] and long trot for a while. You're not pulling him or picking on him to jog slow."

Analyze the Response

Your horse teaches you. By observing his reactions, you can apply equine psychology to figure out the cause of resistance. Once you identify the reason and modify a situation, you'll change the response.

Trainers say that a horse's primary motivations are fear, social order, laziness, and food. A frightened animal reverts to its primary defense to run from a threat. You can habituate him to a stimulus so he accepts a sight or sound that would normally frighten him.

Because your horse naturally seeks a leader, you've placed yourself high on the pecking order. Even though most equines are basically lazy and will evade work, you exert authority. When you tell him to do something, he accepts your dominance and submits.

When he doesn't behave as you expect, you take command and think through a problem. Why did he do what he did?

Pat Parelli has explained four scenarios of a horse's response: "He does the right thing for the right reason, and you reward him. He does the wrong thing for the right reason, and you correct him. He does the right thing for the wrong reason, and you correct him. He does the wrong thing for the wrong reason — I might get strong with that."

You're responsible for your horse's actions. Instead of blaming him, first consider what you did or didn't do.

Instructor Andy Moorman has said: "No matter what happens, it's up to you to have to change it. You take the blame on yourself, and you keep working on your own ideals and goals. If you want to be good at riding, you have to criticize yourself. When something goes wrong, you ask, 'What happened? Where did I lose it? Where did I fail to do the right thing?' And you don't let that happen again."

By changing your habits, you can teach your horse to perform as you want. You've identified the cause, and you seek the solution.

Arabian trainer Jim Porcher has explained what he tells riders about getting responses to their cues: "You ask the horse the first time, and it could be you or the horse. You ask him the second time, and it's your fault because you weren't strong enough. The third time you ask him, that's the time you get serious."

Visualize the Response

Scrutinize riders to observe their horses' body language. What does the horse tell you about the rider's cues? Does he move freely forward and appear soft and relaxed? Do you ever see the rider "block" the horse's forward motion, so the horse gaps his mouth and wrings his tail?

Any horse should move "on the bit" or on the aids, so he travels smoothly in balance. Andy Moorman notes the challenge of understanding this concept. "Most of the riders I teach aren't far enough along to be able to put a horse on the bit. You need to take enough feel to collect a horse, but not be stiff and rigid so you lose the feel, or break what I call the circle of energy."

Although Western riders don't always ride on contact, with a straight line from the hand to the bit, the horse should move forward willingly. Like a dressage horse, the Western horse engages his hindquarters to propel himself forward. When he's active behind, he becomes round and drives up underneath himself. He moves with his body weight distributed equally on both ends.

Horses don't naturally carry themselves this way under saddle. When you watch them move, you'll see many go "on the forehand," or "strung out." They tend to carry more weight on the shoulder rather than on the hip — they travel with more weight on the forehand.

The hindquarters have two kinds of power: the ability to carry weight, and propulsion. Blending these two forces produces the horse that moves in balance.

In all forms of riding, the equestrian aims to get the horse to work from the hindquarters forward. The rider encourages the animal, "Engage the hindquarters to carry your weight and propel yourself forward."

A horse moving this way performs in balance. He lessens the burden on the shoulders, and this reduces the pounding on the front legs. Because he naturally weighs more in his front end, shifting weight backward equalizes the concussion. He moves lightly and softly, pleasing the eye through an athletic appearance.

You achieve this by transferring the weight back, driving the horse into the bridle with your leg. You guide him with light rein aids so he's "soft in the face." You can cue him to collect (gather himself) or extend, so he willingly adjusts his stride, speed, and direction. He can gallop, stop, and turn. If you're chasing a cow or running barrels, he should be able to shift his weight safely, at any speed.

"The horse always moves from behind forward," trainer Jon Higginson has explained. He continues: "You don't concentrate on bridling your horse so much that you forget about the hind end. You keep your horse between your seat and your hands, and you'll always have his hind end driving forward."

While guiding the horse, the horseman does not move aggressively. She cues firmly, without force or anger. Pat Parelli has described this as being "passively persistent. You cause your idea to become the horse's idea, but you understand his idea first."

To succeed as a horseman, you refine your aids. "You have to ride the whole horse," Jim Porcher has noted. "It takes a lot of leg and back, and subtlety with the hands."

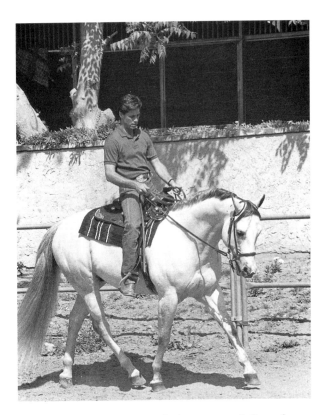

The equestrian aims to get the horse to work from the hindquarters forward. A horse moving this way performs in balance, reducing the pounding on the front legs.

Educate Your Hands

Expect to take time learning how to use your aids. Although skilled riders don't rely on their hands, as a novice you'll focus on overcoming a natural tendency to grab with the reins for security.

"It's important not to take hold and choke a horse down," trainer Gary Ferguson has said. "But it's natural. A person's first instinct is to grab and pull back."

Respect your horse by not over-riding him. Aim to balance contact with lightness. When you need to apply pressure, make a smooth adjustment and ask quietly.

You're seeking softness and artistry in the way you handle the horse. If he responds to one pound of pressure, you apply no more than that.

You want to keep him soft at the poll, or willingly yielding to pressure. "The horse must be able to break over the poll and be soft," Arizona trainer Tony Boit has pointed out. "I feel the front legs, the lower jaw, everything is connected to the poll. If the horse is stiff in the poll, he's going to be stiff all over."

Casey Hinton has noted: "You want the horse to always give his chin. If he doesn't surrender his chin to you, he's not surrendering his body, his back, or anything else. When I pick up the reins, I always want the horse to yield."

Know when to give, to loosen the rein, and when to take, to shorten or "bump." You also need to understand how much pressure to apply, a pull or a bump. (A bump doesn't mean a jerk, or a sudden "chop" that you apply with force.) For example, a pull with a snaffle could mean taking a feel of the mouth and squeezing with your legs. When you feel him round underneath himself and lighten, reward him by sitting still.

You don't want your horse to hollow out, or sink his back and fall onto the forehand. In a transition, you might feel this if you overflex him, using too much hand so he comes behind the bit. Increase leg pressure to drive him forward, and lift your inside hand slightly.

Instructor Larry Gimple has explained: "Sensitivity comes with savvy. The rider finally gets a feel of the horse, but she has to establish it herself. It can't be taught. You have to know the proper length of rein, when to bump or not to bump."

"You've got to adapt to the horse's ability," is the way Texas trainer Nancy Cahill has explained it. "A good hand is what you're working toward all the time. How to use the hands, and when to quit, are probably most difficult. You learn timing and feel that don't come into words."

When practicing, most Western riders ride two-handed, with a rein in each hand. Hold the reins so a half-inch will shorten enough to take a feel. Check the position of your upper arms, which shouldn't be behind the vertical.

Learn the difference between two types of hands, the fixed and the following hand. When you ride on light contact, you'll usually adopt the "following" hand.

Find contact without pulling or hanging on the horse's mouth. You want a feel between your hand and the mouth, to help the horse. If your hands bounce, practice holding them steady by putting your little fingers on the saddle's pommel. Hold them there, no matter what your body does.

With the reins too loose, the unfinished horse has a tendency to drop his shoulders. The finished horse should move into a gait, and when you drop your hand to give him a loose rein, he maintains his impulsion and frame.

You want your horse to stay in position between the two reins, so he follows his nose. You rein him into a turn by guiding, not steering. Aim for light, subtle use of the reins when two-handing or neck reining.

Educate Your Legs

A horseman rides more off the legs and seat than off the hand. Learning this principle requires you to take command and resist grabbing first and legging second. You can't balance a 1,000-pound horse through pulling his head.

Andy Moorman has noted a tendency among novice riders. "If the horse fails to respond, the rider typically responds with her hand instead of

To apply the leg aid, slide the lower leg behind the cinch, and use a soft squeeze.

her leg first. It's a habit. She clutches instead of drives, and then she's in trouble. You have to train yourself to react with your leg first.

"Whatever you feel you need to do with your hand, you need to do instead with your leg. If you start to use your leg in place of your hand, pretty soon your hand can be still and soft. Most people with bad hands don't have an educated leg."

You learn to use your leg independently of your hand, but this doesn't imply that you throw the horse away with the hand. Your hand is ready to support while you push him with your legs. Your leg controls his legs. It cues him to move from the hindquarters, and it keeps him "in front of" your leg.

Even when you back up, you ask with the leg. The horse has to shift his weight back to move in reverse. California Arabian trainer Tom Sapp has explained: "Make sure you drive to the bridle, then bring him off the bit. Don't gag him back without

The Horseman's Tools: Bit and Spur

Your tools will teach, control, reinforce, and refine your horse's responses. The value of any tool depends on your attitude.

Because you want the horse to respond to less pressure, use a mild bit. Master trainers rely on the snaffle, and return to it to reinforce skills.

Pat Parelli has advised using the snaffle. The milder, direct action of this bit avoids causing fear. "The snaffle is for lateral flexion. The plain snaffle is ancient and proven. You don't need anything more."

Pick a spur that matches you and your horse.

Trainer Harold Farren has recommended only the plain snaffle. He says: "Because the horse tends to move toward pressure, he'll just push more against the action of a strong bit, like the twisted wire. I've found only one spot on a horse's body that isn't affected this way — the recess under the chin. This spot isn't utilized during schooling with the snaffle bit."

"Use the snaffle to get your end results," Casey Hinton has advised. He prefers the snaffle because the horse can feel the cue and the reward. "It's harder to train to get the result with the snaffle, but you have a better final product."

You will probably show your horse in a curb bit, which can make him respond stiffly. Some horses learn to fear the curb and will push against it if the rider allows no release. "It's a tool of refinement, but you must be more delicate to produce a more delicate response," Parelli has advised.

The spur is an extension, an aid that refines your leg cue. You touch the horse with the spur only if he ignores a squeeze from your legs, and then a bump with your calf. Don't jab or prod, but nudge or roll the rowel lightly. The horse learns to listen to your suggestion.

Pick a spur with a shank to match you and your horse. If you have long legs, you might need a longer shank to reach the horse's side. Choose a shorter shank if you're short, so you won't "grab" the horse too high.

asking him to collect, or he'll start backing off the forehand instead of the rear."

Use your leg so the horse engages his hind foot first, at every gait. Harold Farren has noted: "To lope, the horse has to engage his inside hind foot to the ground and get it under him. That puts him on the front axis of the hip, so he can move off the inside hind and start loping on 'the short stride' [not strung out]. By always engaging that hind foot first, he will respond to the lope cue without trotting in the transition."

With engagement, the horse won't drag his hip or fall into an incorrect, four-beat lope. His driving hip supports his forehand and your weight.

To use your leg, drop it back behind the cinch so your horse can feel it. In some cases, you'll squeeze with both legs, and other times you'll use only one, or one more strongly than the other. Hold your legs still while you ride, unless you're applying a definite aid. If you continually tap against the sides every step, you can make him "dead" to your leg.

Your leg needs to feel strong, yet not rigid or clinging to the horse. A strong leg is a controlled leg, where you can apply the appropriate pressure. You can strengthen your leg position by riding without stirrups. This improves your balance, as you rely on your seat as a base.

Use your leg with proper timing. Your leg indicates the cue before your hand. When you want to round your horse, squeeze lightly with both legs so he moves up to your hand. Aim to increase the pressure slightly on your inside leg, to move him up to the outside rein. Your fingers feel him seek the rein, and you release the leg pressure.

If you need to reinforce your leg aid, bump with the calf. Your pressure in leg and hand match in intensity — follow a firm leg with an increased rein cue. Lighten leg and rein to teach the horse to respond with greater sensitivity.

Tony Boit has described leg pressure as a cue and release. "Don't hold the leg. Leg, get it off, leg, get it off. It's like a punching bag. The degree of the punch is the degree of how much the horse listens to you."

To turn, press with the leg, either inside or outside depending on your horse's training. Instead of using the hand, you indicate the direction with your leg. Press the leg in rhythm with the horse.

The amount of leg pressure also influences the horse. A soft, massaging squeeze can gather him without making him increase his speed. When he willingly steps forward from behind, you feel a wave of energy, not necessarily an acceleration.

Andy Moorman has commented: "If you use your legs without involving your body, then you only change the horse's legs. You won't change the horse's rhythm. The horse will lengthen his stride, but he won't increase his rhythm if you use the leg properly. The horse collects, but he doesn't speed up. If you use your leg incorrectly, the horse will speed up."

Training Exercises

Warm up at the walk. Andy Moorman has said: "I like to lengthen the walk on a loose rein to begin with, until the horse comes through and swings his back. He says, 'Okay, I'm ready.' If you always start that way, then he'll accept what you do."

Practice adjusting your horse's stride, beginning with the walk. Instructor Terry McCutcheon has said: "Using your legs, you impulse the horse into a longer, extended stride. Then keep the horse balanced, so he's in a position where he travels equally in his stride. One step leads to another, and the basics from a walk apply to the trot and lope."

From the lengthened walk, use your legs to ask your horse to gather himself for a more collected walk. Move into the trot, lengthen the trot, and move back to the jog.

When you're moving at a faster gait, try using your seat to slow into a downward transition. Exaggerate your weight cues, to allow your horse to have time to respond to them before you use any rein pressure.

How he moves from the lope to the halt points out the quality of your horse's connection between forehand and hindquarters. Jim Porcher has commented: "Stabilize the lope with your outside leg. To halt, use your calf to push the horse to your hands. Don't let him brace into it, but pick him up with your hand."

Casey Hinton has explained a simple exercise to use in the downward transition, from the lope to the halt. Use this in conjunction with his suppling exercises, described later in this chapter.

The halt reinforces the basic message of "Surrender." You look for the horse to give to you with his poll.

Say "whoa" once, then as you repeat it, put your rein hand straight down as you reprimand. Take out the slack, and pull back to your hip. Leave your hand down, and don't raise it at all during the transition.

"Concentrate on a more perfect head position, not how quick the horse responds," cautioned Hinton. "Don't pull on the reins too soon. It takes a horse longer to digest a thought and respond than it does a person. Your horse needs two seconds to react to the whoa.

"When you take his head, [you want your horse] to say, 'How much?' not, 'Make me!'" Hinton has explained. "Don't quit until the horse gives in to you."

Backing up can help the horse stop, when used carefully. Hinton doesn't rely on this movement as punishment. "He can start thinking about being punished for backing up." If your horse "trickles" to a stop, use an equal amount of backing steps as a reprimand. For example, you ask for the stop, and he lopes four steps after your cue. Back him up four steps, then lope again.

Precision in Your Aids

Knowing how to use aids to influence the horse distinguishes the horseman from the passenger. The horseman performs a change of gait with his horse's hindquarters engaged and both shoulders lifted. His horse moves gracefully in any direction and bends equally to right and left.

Your horse might carry himself well on a straight line but fall apart on turns or circles and lose the equal weight distribution between inside and outside, front and rear. Practicing arcs will help you coordinate your aids to shift your horse's body right or left, to move the shoulder out and then in. When arcing, press with your inside leg to keep

Wrong

Right

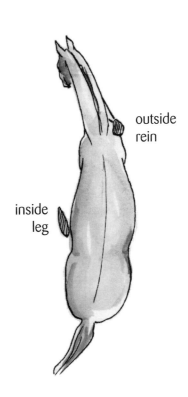

outside rein

inside leg

Practicing arcs will help you coordinate your aids. Press with your inside leg, and use your outside rein, as diagonal aids. The body follows the forehand. Don't let the horse "rubberneck."

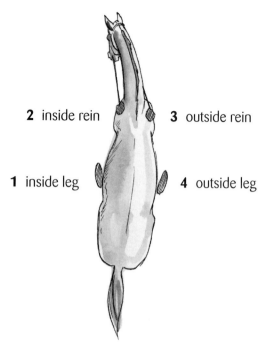

2 inside rein   **3** outside rein

1 inside leg   **4** outside leg

In the lope, get the horse soft on the inside leg and inside rein. Then close the outside rein so the shoulder doesn't leak out. Finally, push in the hip with your outside leg.

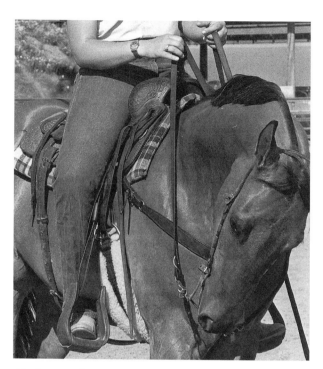

Used in combination, the brace rein and flexion rein cue the horse to bend correctly, with a relaxed neck.

the ribcage lifted. Your leg aid assists your inside hand and pushes the shoulder out and around. Remember that the body follows the forehand, and don't let the horse "rubberneck."

Using diagonal aids — inside leg and outside rein together — can help. Andy Moorman has used the image of doors on the horse's shoulders and hips. "You can't let the doors come open. You keep the horse balanced between your two reins and two legs. You always have something going on with both hands and both legs. One may be passive, another active, and that changes."

In the lope, Moorman teaches riders to focus on the sequence of footfalls and think of the aids as a "U" that follows the horse's body. "Start with your inside leg, inside rein, outside rein, outside leg. With the diagonal aids, you have to get the horse's outside leg under him, because that's the leg that he's going to rock back on to step up. Get him soft on the inside leg and inside rein. Then close the outside rein so the shoulder doesn't leak out, so he will listen to your outside leg. The final thing you do is push the hip in with the outside leg. And the minute he starts to pick up the

inside hind leg, then you have to increase with your inside leg to make that hind leg come deep under the horse. It's just a set of doing this, over and over."

Practice isolating the horse's front or hind end. Here you cue the horse to move his fore- or hindquarters only. He moves his front end around his rear, or his rear end around the front. This exercise helps you coordinate your aids, and helps your horse to balance and connect from the hindquarters to your hand.

You use two reins here, called the "brace" rein and "flexion" rein. The brace rein is a combination of outside leg and hand, to steady the horse; the flexion rein is a combination of inside leg and hand to flex the horse to the inside. Used in combination, your aids cue the horse to bend correctly, with a relaxed neck. He moves his shoulders, keeping them lifted so his forehand remains light. A dropped shoulder means he shifted more weight onto his forehand and won't move in balance.

Practice isolations at the standstill, which results in a turn on the forehand or hindquarters.

For the turn on the haunches, use your outside leg and hand as the brace rein. Apply inside leg and hand as the flexion rein. Your outside leg cues the horse to move. He bends around your inside leg, which maintains him in balance and keeps the shoulder up. Coordinate the pressure so you don't overbend.

In a correct arc, you should be able to see the horse's inside eye and ear. You should feel his balance shifted to the rear, and see that the shoulders are up. If you feel the inside shoulder get heavy, raise your inside hand to pick up the rein and bump the mouth.

With your outside leg, you can tell the horse to move his shoulder over. Your inside leg positions the hindquarters, encouraging him to bunch up and move underneath himself.

For the horse with a weak loin that resists engagement, Jim Porcher suggests combining the turn on the haunches with the downward transition. He coaches: "When you halt, use your outside leg to make the horse move away from the rail. Your leg transfers his weight back to ask him to turn. Hold him to pick him up and make him strengthen himself as he transfers."

The horse might evade your cue by swinging his hindquarters and trying to walk out of the movement. Apply a firmer leg aid to arc him up, so he engages the hindquarters.

"The horse will naturally want to move his rear end, because his weight's on his forehand," says Porcher. "You pick up the front end and move it around the rear end. You have to be light and still have some contact with the horse's face."

Practicing circles will help you improve your bending aids and your control. Circles combine a figure with an animal's body, and a perfect circle is very difficult. The horse must arc his body without resistance.

The circle also can help correct a problem. If your horse is strung out, moving heavily on the forehand, put him in a small circle to collect him. With a more acute bend, you can feel his movement, and he's less able to "cheat" on you. When you feel him moving more from the hindquarters, let him move onto a larger circle.

By practicing circles, you can improve your bending aids and your horse's balance.

You use both reins and both legs in a small circle. The outside rein turns the body. The outside rein is dominant and it regulates the horse's frame.

Pat Parelli has explained: "When you use the outside rein, you're getting a hold of the hindquarters. Pull that rein, and you talk to the hindquarters. Then look where the forequarters go. It's like turning the wheel of a boat, where you turn the wheel and the rudder follows."

You should feel that connection as the outside rein holds the horse going forward yet bent. The inside rein dictates the bend to the inside, or flexion.

Nancy Cahill has told riders to make a perfectly round circle like a figure skater. "See if you can stay in your tracks. It teaches you — you used too much left hand, or too much right, or he dropped a shoulder. The hardest thing for anybody to learn is where every piece of that horse's body is."

Some horses cut in on a circle, or bulge to the outside. Bend the horse to the inside to prevent cutting in, using your inside leg to move the rib cage out. This can produce a bulge, so here your outside rein can receive the bulge, block it, and keep the horse curved in a smooth arc. You should feel him slightly bent, working against the outside rein. He angles his body weight to the outside in order to keep balanced.

Most trainers feel the horse bends in three places — neck, shoulder, and rib cage. The neck and shoulders should be square and lifted. Gary Ferguson has said: "You always move from the hip forward. The shoulders and rib cage definitely have to give to bend away from your leg around the corner. The horse arcs correctly and follows his nose where he's going."

You want to think in terms of your horse as an extension of yourself. He responds to your aids when he's attuned and synchronized to you. He yields to your aids because he wants to, not because you force him.

Suppling the Horse

When you ride your horse, you'll continually remind him to submit to you. Trainers rely on exercises to train the horse to obey with the mind while performing as an athlete.

For that soft feel, you can flex the horse's body and mind. In past centuries, European masters of classical riding used doubling, a training exercise that brings the horse's head back to the saddle or the rider's leg in a willing fashion. This helped the young horse learn submission.

Today the exercise is used mainly in Western riding to help teach a horse to turn quickly. Many trainers use it along a fence line, doubling the horse into the fence so he pivots on his inside hind leg.

At a slower speed, you can follow a three-step program as taught by Casey Hinton. He has used this technique to supple any horse and to control the animal 100 percent.

Step 1

First you ask the horse to surrender his head and lighten the forehand. "The reason for training the head is that it's the horse's steering wheel," explains Hinton. "Everything you teach the head to do, the body has to follow, whether it's stopping,

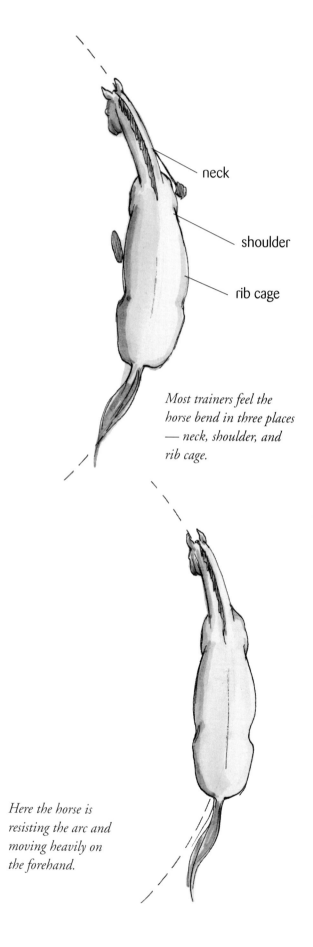

Most trainers feel the horse bend in three places — neck, shoulder, and rib cage.

Here the horse is resisting the arc and moving heavily on the forehand.

spinning, or changing leads. I want to move the front end by telling the head to do it.

"Take the slack out of your left rein, and pull toward your hip. Pull out and back to make the horse's feet step across. Just hold the rein and let him decide."

Lighten your rein hand and keep your fingers soft, without clenching or jiggling the reins. Hinton describes this as "pulling relaxed."

When the horse obeys by moving his nose and near forefoot to the left, flexing to you, immediately pitch the reins to him. Hinton says: "Give the horse slack when he makes the decision because of the pressure. Hold it there until he decides to give in. When your horse starts stepping with his feet, tip your hand down and release. Walk straight forward, make him follow the rein and step across, and walk straight again, so you end up doing a circle."

You must wait, holding the rein, until the horse gives to you and steps. Tell him that he moved away from pressure, so the pressure went away. Hinton cautions: "Don't force it! Don't bump it! Just hold the rein, and let your horse rock his head and bump the bit until he responds, then take away the command. He'll give in, put his head down, and surrender."

For a 100-percent response, you want to see the poll lower and feel the feet stepping across as the horse swings his shoulder. However, your horse might cheat by moving the head and not the forehand, or swinging his hip instead of his shoulder. Any such response shows you that you control only a small portion of the horse.

What about the horse that steps without dipping his poll? "Take his head all the way to the side, and get more forward impulsion on a larger circle. A horse that just turns will drop his shoulders at the lope."

Forward movement also improves the response in Step 1. Here you can add a squeeze with the calf. Hinton says: "I want to move the front end by telling the head to do it, so I use the leg more as a reprimand than a cue. If you don't need the leg, don't use it.

"Make the horse's feet go better with his head. Use your outside leg and speed up the front end.

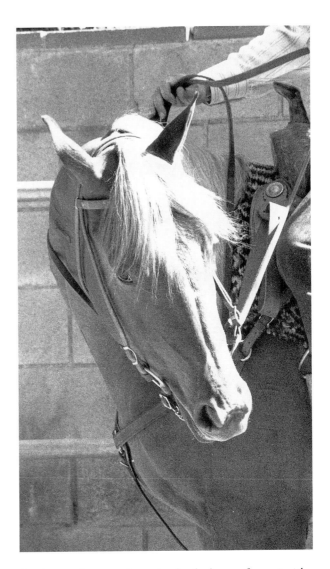

In the suppling exercise, take the slack out of your inside rein and pull toward your hip to make the horse's feet step across. Hold the rein and let him decide to move. Don't force it.

Drive the horse forward on a bigger circle. While you continue walking, get the chin a little bit at a time. Make that head move, to come to you and to flex to your side."

Your horse discovers how to avoid the pull of the rein. "The only spot where I leave the horse alone is when his head is correct. Every time he straightens, I take his head back. He finds the spot where it's easiest to surrender, and when I leave him alone, he stays in the position I want."

*Teach the horse to shove his shoulder to the outside —
you teach him to move out, still stepping across
with the front feet.*

Step 2

Teach the horse to "push away," or shove his
shoulder to the outside. With his moving forward,
you flex the body and teach him to flex his poll.

You teach him to move out, still stepping
across with the front feet. Hinton: "At this point
you're going to use your other rein more. The inside rein's going to push, and the outside rein
pulls a little bit. Pick up your inside rein, and
push both hands across the neck to the outside.
You want the horse to move between the bit,
between the reins."

The horse steps his feet to the outside. When
you circle right, you should feel him stepping his
left foot over the right.

To keep forward momentum, experiment with
the amount and timing of leg pressure. Look for

your horse to appear relaxed. His ears should tell
you he's waiting for you to tell him what to do.
"Every time you get a result, give a reward," Hinton
stresses. "Teach your horse to push away, then leave
him alone. If you constantly pull, or bury your
hands on your horse, pretty soon he'll push right
back. You want him to soften, because you're going to release that pressure."

Use this shoulder-out exercise as a progression,
and work in both directions for a light, supple
attitude. Even if the shoulders move only one step,
quit asking, relax, and allow your horse to walk forward on a slack rein. Next time, try to get his chin
to flex a little more, and increase the exercise to two
steps. If you get three steps at the walk, begin working at a jog.

Look for the horse to flatten his neck when you
take hold. When he resists with his poll, you lose
control. Hinton advises: "When your horse gets
away in his face, he won't react with his feet. Take
your time, but make it definite. Look where he
hangs his head."

If you're tracking right, your horse's hip might
drift left. Apply your left leg and take the head further with your pull and release.

Try to increase the intensity of the response.
"Make your message more extreme with forward
motion, which will get the response for you," Hinton says. "Dramatize your cue and reward, and see
how much more flexibility you get."

Step 3

Here you change the direction of the shoulder on the circle, to push it to the inside. Tracking left, use your right leg and right rein to shove
the shoulder. Your horse should respond by moving
on two tracks, limbering his backbone.

Hinton notes: "Only get a couple steps, and
drop the reins when the horse moves his shoulders.
After you do it in a circle, let him relax and go on
a straight line."

Adjust your timing to the reaction. Decide if
you need to slow it down to calm a nervous horse.

Keep forward motion because with too much
rein pressure the horse might back up. Hinton explains: "The horse has the willingness to surrender

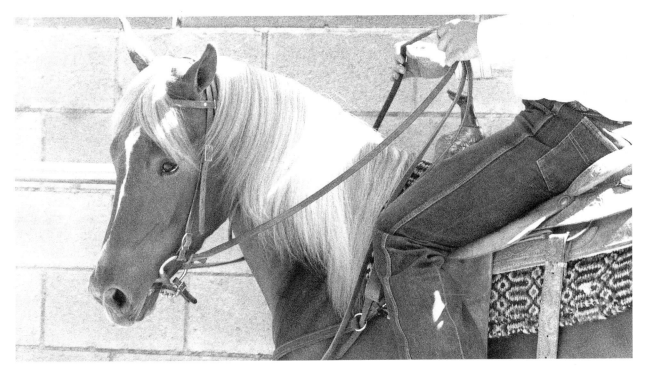

Apply agitation with both reins for direct flexion. You want the horse to move between the bit, between the reins. His ears should tell you he's waiting for you to tell him what to do.

because you release the pressure and allow him to walk forward."

In Steps 2 and 3, you might encounter what Hinton calls a "sticky spot," or a slight resistance going one direction. Concentrate on this weaker side so you achieve equal control on both right and left sides.

Lifelong Learning

Becoming a horseman means work. Trainer Sue Cummins has compared riding to life. "It's a challenge. What is life but one obstacle course after another? It causes you to move to the next level of who you are. It's fun, the fun of learning, self-esteem, building confidence, and overcoming the obstacles."

Western riding poses a challenge unique to horsemanship. Gill Swarbrick has compared Western riding to dressage. "People don't realize that Western is harder. The horse has to be trained to work on a minimum amount of contact. You don't just get packed around!"

Change the direction of the shoulder on the circle, to push it to the inside. When tracking left, use your right leg and right rein to push the shoulder to the inside.

Trainer Art Gaytan agrees, comparing the bits and seats. "Both disciplines use a snaffle bit, and later as the horse becomes proficient, both go to almost exactly the same curb bit of a 5 to 2 ratio. The seat is the same, straight up and down in Western and dressage. But the Western rider asks his horse to perform and then maintain that gait until he asks it to change. You shouldn't have to move the horse up, or slow him down."

With the horse moving on minimum contact, the classical equestrian principles apply: *rhythm, relaxation, connection, engagement, straightness,* and *collection.* Horsemen the world over pursue this natural progression.

7

Trail Riding Pleasures

The beckoning trail inspires you to saddle up, humming the old Roy Rogers tune, "Happy trails to you. . . ." What delights lie ahead, as you and your horse tour the world beyond the barn. As you develop your horsemanship skills, riding outside brings you new pleasures to share with your equine partner. Together you'll wander along quiet paths and canter across grassy slopes or deserted beaches. After a long uphill climb, you'll arrive at the summit and survey the landscape on the other side. Trail riding offers a range of benefits besides being fun. The world looks different on horseback. You can explore familiar and unfamiliar sights. You and your horse share the adventure, as he travels with a purpose. Most animals enjoy the relaxation of wandering along paths.

You can experience trail riding just about anywhere — around the neighborhood, on dedicated trails, along a waterway, through a pasture, or across public lands. Your trails can be solitary excursions or social occasions. With fellow riders, everyone savors a closeness with nature while riding at a leisurely pace.

Trail riding can help condition your horse's muscles and bone density, so he's ready to tackle more strenuous work. A workout intended to muscle him up — to "work his tail off" — can change his behavior by releasing tension or boredom. Choose varied footing and terrain for your travels, such as riding in deep footing like the sand of a dry riverbed. Riding up hills helps settle a nervous horse.

Unpredictable footing can teach the horse to watch where he's going. If you ride in the desert and have to cross a patch of rocky ground, you encourage him to drop his head to pick his way through. Mountainous terrain lets him find his own way of going, as he puts his feet down correctly and maintains his natural balance.

Ride Type	Location	Description	Organizer
Informal day ride	Town, suburbs, country, wilderness	Ride for fun Ride to a destination Ride in a loop, from start to finish, or meet at an arranged pickup point	Riders
Organized day ride	Country, wilderness	Planned itinerary Sponsoring group charges entry fees or horse rental	Riding club Breed organization Wrangler at guest ranch or resort
Overnight ride	Country, wilderness	Horse camping Pack gear on horses Gear trucked to sites	Riding club Breed organization Trail guide Wilderness outfitter Riders

Work up to such challenges, because not all horses are coordinated on the trail. In steep, uneven terrain, a few animals will stumble and have trouble maintaining their footing.

CURTIS MARTIN

A trail-wise horse is surefooted, nimble, and balanced.

The Trail-Wise Horse

A capable trail horse usually moves with a long stride and carries a naturally low headset. He should be rugged with strong bones, but he does not have to be heavily muscled. An overly muscular type may not move as freely over rough terrain. A horse should have prominent withers to hold the saddle in place. Mules tend to have low withers, so a crupper helps keep the saddle from sliding forward. For hill climbing, many horsemen look for an animal with powerful hindquarters.

You want your trail horse to be surefooted and to negotiate any incline or uneven footing. Look for feet that are large enough to support the horse's weight and to "grab on" in a crisis. Mules, famed for their agility, often excel when you're going "down trail."

The trail-wise animal is nimble and sensible. He knows where to place his feet and how to pick his way deftly over loose gravel, jagged shale, or slick granite. When traveling along a tough section of trail, he carefully maintains his balance.

You could be climbing along a pile of rocks or traversing a narrow ledge. On a tortuous path, this equine athlete twists and turns to keep his feet in place. Because he's broke for the trail, he surmounts obstacles with a casual attitude.

The trail-wise mount trusts you and goes where you guide him, regardless of the behavior of his equine companions. He isn't herd bound and will work alone or in company, traveling at the front, rear, or middle of a group.

A safe trail horse remains calm and responds instantly to your aids, no matter what. He stops and stands where you want. When you ask, he slows to a quiet walk or moves at a brisk six-mile-per-hour stride. He doesn't rear, bolt, kick, or spook, and he'll tolerate the sound of gunshot and the smell of game you ask him to carry or drag. When you have to tie him up at a lunch stop or overnight, he'll cock a hind foot and relax. You could even praise this horse as politically correct, because he respects the environment. When you tie him to a tree limb, he doesn't paw the ground to damage a tree's root system. A perfect trail horse will ground tie and wait till you return. (A pretty good one will stand tied to a bush.) A trail horse may not express his love for you, but he won't abandon you, either. If he finds himself loose, he waits for you to find him. (He wouldn't consider hightailing it for home!)

The Misbehaving Horse

You may find yourself on a mount that lacks the above trail-wise attributes. Your horse might be broke — until you join friends for a trail ride. If you're an authoritative rider with a less-than-ideal mount, you can still enjoy excursions. Most wrecks on the trail involve equine misbehaviors, such as kicking, spooking, or being barn sour. You can figure out the reasons for each action, and prevent misbehavior or retrain the horse.

Your partner might never kick, except when you're riding in a group. Then he decides to dominate his neighbors, especially if they incite him by "tailgating."

Fellow riders won't welcome your kicker, as a flying hoof aimed at another horse endangers the other rider as well. The targeted animal dodges, and the hoof impacts upon your friend's knee, shin, or foot. Ouch!

If you ride alertly, you can discourage a horse from kicking his buddies. Remain cautious at all times, on the trail and at rest stops. If anyone approaches the kicking zone, warn the person with a verbal, "Watch out; he kicks." Or, tie the traditional red ribbon around the top of your horse's tail.

Watch out for other horses kicking or biting yours, too. Keep a distance — at least a horse's length — from the horse ahead of you, and stay away from tailgaters.

Pay attention to your horse's attitude. If his ears go back and you see he's on the defensive, correct an impending kick with your voice and legs, or even a crack of the whip. If you feel him shift his weight forward or to one side, reprimand him firmly before he lifts one or both hind feet.

The spooker is the most common terror of the trail. Realize that an unpredictable sight or sound can "booger" any horse. The intensity of his reaction depends on the fearsomeness of the object and the horse's athletic ability.

You can't predict spookiness until you begin riding outside. Many horses will never shy in a familiar environment, but they transform into "fraidy cats" 50 feet down the road. As you explore different roads and paths, you'll learn by experience which sights, sounds, or even smells strike fear into your horse's heart.

Expect him to question such common sights as dogs, pigs, cows, sheep, trash, trash cans, flapping clothes on clotheslines, railroad tracks, and helicopters. When you travel to more remote environments, you could encounter backpackers, mountain bikers, burros, llamas, or large rocks that resemble bears.

Because you're the leader, you determine how to guide your horse through a scary situation. At his clinics, trainer John Lyons teaches horses to stand and face a threat, without turning away or

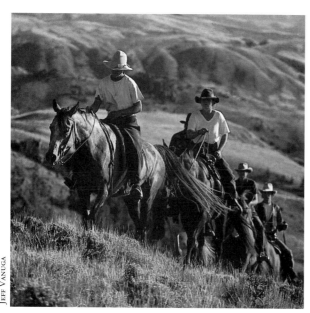

Walking uphill, the lead rider keeps an eye on his horse's ears and helps the horse by shifting his weight forward.

running from it. In many cases, you can comfort your horse with a calm pat and by saying, "Easy."

Equestrian authority Linda Tellington-Jones has taught ways to help the horse overcome his fear of a common terror like water. Through using her Tellington-Jones Equine Awareness Methods (TTEAM) groundwork exercises, you can teach your horse to deal with fear of the unknown. He learns to think rather than react while you calmly let him cope.

Watch your horse's ears along the trail. This is how he will alert you to wildlife, other domestic animals, and people as you travel. When you see him intently focus his ears toward something, remain confident and cue him to continue moving forward.

If you haven't done your homework and trained him to overcome a specific fear, you can take two approaches when he becomes spooked. Some experts suggest riding your horse up to the supposed threat; others contend you should ignore it and continue normally. Whatever you do, breathe normally and continue to ride assertively. Don't convey anxiety to your horse. Never allow him to use the object as an opportunity to back up or to turn around and return to the barn. Continue moving forward, even if you have to go out of your way, or, as the absolute last resort, dismount and lead him past it. (Tip: Try

distracting him by cueing for a shoulder in. Or, make him rein back, still progressing in the direction you have set.)

Shying endangers both of you. If your seat isn't secure, a whirling horse can dump you before you realize what spooked him. Also, he could slip and lose his footing, or slam into a hazardous object such as a fence or car. In the back country, this character could even fall off a narrow ledge, far from the search and rescue team. (Now you see why trail riding is so risky and why protective headgear is so important.)

You can outride spooks by developing a strong seat and predicting your horse's responses. Remind him that you remain in control and that he must obey your commands despite his fear.

You can desensitize him about a persistent phobia by surrounding him with the very objects he fears. You could stable him temporarily beside a pen of potbellied pigs, hang plastic bags beside his corral, or ride a noisy motorbike back and forth past the stall.

Hopefully you'll never ride a barn-sour horse — one that doesn't like to leave the barn. Any horse will want to hurry home, seeking rest and food, but a brisk walk should be the fastest gait you permit.

Ride for Credit

Several breed associations have recognized the numbers of horsemen who ride for pleasure. The American Quarter Horse Association (AQHA), American Paint Horse Association (APHA), and Appaloosa Horse Club (ApHC) sponsor programs that award you for the riding miles you record.

Open to members of the association, the program gives you credit for specific achievement levels, calculated by the hours you accrue. You complete a log to qualify for awards. For example, the Appaloosa Saddle Log Awards give you a patch after you complete 100 hours riding a registered Appaloosa.

Trail Equitation

Ride in a balanced seat, so you can move with your horse. Usually you'll ride on a somewhat loose rein or with light contact, so your horse carries his head and neck at his natural balance point.

Trail riding involves climbing and descending slopes, hills, or even mountains. Your mount has to carry your combined weights uphill. Check your cinch again before scaling a steep hill. As you start up a grade, help your horse by maintaining your balance. Get your weight forward off his loins, without leaning forward from the waist so you crouch over the withers. This can overload his neck and forehand, inhibiting his impulsion to pull up the hill. And if you sit back too far, you'll put too much weight on the hindquarters.

To ride at the ideal angle, sit over the horse's center of balance. As a guide, look at any trees alongside you, and match your backbone to the vertical trunks. Push down in the stirrups so you shove your feet forward in line with the girth. You'll avoid hitting your feet against the horse's stifle or gaskin, and you'll find this position helps him negotiate the incline.

Avoid hanging on to the saddle horn, because you increase the pressure on the girth if you pull on the horn. Grab the mane if you need to balance yourself.

Don't let your horse race uphill — teach him to conserve his energy by stopping partway up the grade to rest. When you stop, pick a place where you can turn him right or left, so he stands level. On a long, steep grade, you may make several short stops so your horse can catch his breath.

Riding uphill rewards you with a sense of achievement. Yet what goes up must come down. When you start downhill, keep contact so the horse doesn't increase his speed or lose his balance on the grade. He should keep his feet and hocks under him.

Again maintain your weight over the horse's center of gravity, and stand slightly in the stirrups so you're light in the saddle. Your seat should just

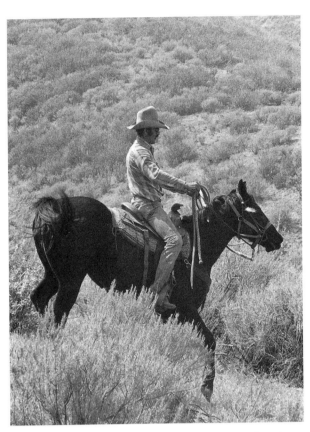

To ride downhill at an ideal angle, sit over the horse's center of balance. Push down in the stirrups so you move your feet forward in line with the girth.

brush the saddle, so you're in what hunt-seat riders call the "two-point" position.

Place your free hand on the saddle's pommel, or the horn, and hold your weight steady by keeping your ankles bent so your heels are down. You absorb the concussion in your legs.

With most of your weight in the stirrups, keep your legs close to the horse without gripping. If you tense up, your body will start to sway. This could put your horse off balance down a steep hill.

As your horse tilts down the incline, he drops his head and neck. Those ears just seem to disappear!

You'll naturally want to lean way back to keep from going over his head. Resist this tendency, because you'll make it harder for your horse to keep his balance. If you plant your seat firmly in the saddle, his hind feet will dig further into the ground. He may start to scoot down the grade, sliding on his hocks, because he can't get his hind legs out from under himself. Watch for difficult inclines on slippery ground, such as slick rocks or deep sand. If you do feel your horse slide or tilt dangerously, be ready to bail out. You don't want to roll down the hill with him, because you could end up underneath him at the bottom.

Watch that your feet don't swing too far forward or back. You can use an alternating leg to counterbalance the motion — put slightly more weight in the opposite stirrup at each step. When your horse steps forward with his left front leg, put weight on your right stirrup.

Few riders sit too far forward downhill, but this can overbalance the horse's forehand. He can stumble or even fall.

Trail Smarts

With your determined attitude and balanced seat, you'll bond with your horse as you ride the trails together. He learns to trust you outside. In a demanding situation, you decide whether to continue, go around, or turn back. When you feel him hesitate, you only push forward if you know it's safe to do so. When you ride bravely, you communicate your attitude to your horse. You're "driving," and he goes where you guide him. Brave doesn't mean careless, however. Combine common sense with forward motion. You can learn trail smarts from experienced riders and trail-wise horses. Ride with a group, and follow the lead of the best rider or the trail guide. If you ride at a guest ranch or on a rented horse, pay attention to how the horse handles himself.

On any trail, the first rule is to watch where you're going. Scan the landscape ahead so you're prepared for any changes in the earth below your horse's feet, on each side, and above your head. When you ride under a tree, be sure you can duck under branches without scraping your back. Lean forward and hold onto your hat.

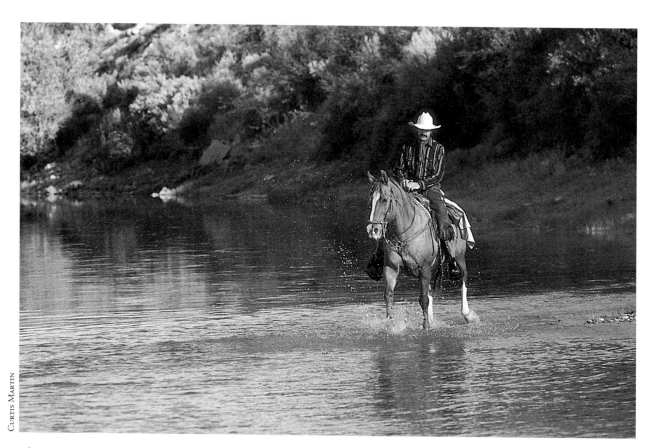

If your horse fears crossing water, start him across a shallow creek so he learns to trust you and the water.

On a narrow trail, you'll navigate through the tight space. Rein your horse around brush, scanning ahead for gaps. You might have to take your feet out of one or both stirrups when you move next to a bank or large rock. You don't want to get your foot stuck between your horse and a rock, or brush your knee against a snake sunning itself.

Besides watching for snakes, be ready for pheasants or rabbits that can surprise both you and your horse. Other natural irritants can include ticks (which land on you or your horse when you touch bushes) and the temptations of plants at your horse's level. Don't let him grab at trees or brush. This is an irritating habit, and he could possibly eat a poisonous plant.

Horses must get used to crossing unfamiliar terrain, but it's your job to check for the footing. Don't push fast through deep sand, and inspect wet or loose footing. In a marshy area, watch for quicksand and sinkholes. If the ground ahead seems boggy, consider going around on firmer terrain. The two of you weigh 1,100 to 1,300 pounds, and that weight can sink much faster than you alone. Could you rescue your horse if he became trapped? Never cross a cattle guard. A horse can easily catch his foot and find himself in a deathtrap.

A horse raised on flat ground may fear crossing a ditch or arroyo. When you encounter a steep ditch, keep him moving but not plunging forward to try to jump the gap. Keep him facing the obstacle and cue him to walk forward. By your attitude, you let him know there's nothing to be afraid of.

Consider your momentum in such situations. Increased speed could carry you down steep terrain, but will you be able to get back up?

Many horses fear crossing water. Because they can't sense the depth of a puddle, stream, or pond, they tend to distrust any water.

Before you cross running water, you have to know its depth and current. If possible, start your horse across a shallow creek with a solid bottom. He learns to trust you and navigate obstacles, and you can move on to more demanding water crossings.

Allow your horse to drink water during these encounters, which also familiarizes him with it. If he's hot, let him drink a reasonable amount, and keep him moving for at least half an hour before you stop, to avoid possible colic from the cold water.

Some horses want to roll in water. If your horse drops his head down and paws, move him forward immediately. An abrupt dunking is no fun, and you could lose control of the animal. Don't take chances if you're unsure. In rough terrain, stay away from the edge of ledges. Stay back from the horse ahead — he could balk, spook, or fall, and you'd be part of the wreck. Judge every obstacle.

Riding through Suburbs

Whenever you ride through a residential or commercial zone, realize that you and your horse are "on stage." Ride with respect toward the inhabitants, and keep a low profile. Crossing through a horseless neighborhood is a privilege, not a right. Polite riding will keep horses welcomed. Ride in single file at a slow gait. (Never ride faster than at a slow jog on pavement.) Stay on the road, not the sidewalk, so you don't interfere with pedestrians.

In a populated area, you risk the embarrassing event of your horse dropping manure. This is probably the reason suburban homeowners and in-town businessmen object to equestrian traffic. In the saddle, you can only apologize if someone complains about your horse's functions.

You'll have more fun riding in less populous neighborhoods, where you can follow a path or trail by the road. Keep your horse along the road, avoiding private property. Never cross a lawn or garden, and don't let your horse nibble hedges, bushes, or trees. Besides leaving shrubbery untouched, this safeguards his health. Many ornamental plants, such as the popular oleander, are poisonous to horses.

Tack, attire, and other items match the purpose and length of your ride. These horsemen are ready for a day in the high country.

If it could hurt the horse, then he has reason to question you next time, and you've lost trust. Trust his judgment too, such as crossing a rickety bridge. A sensible mount recognizes whether or not he can go down a cliff. The trail-wise horse will hesitate, whereas a dull-witted one may not.

Changing weather conditions can also endanger you and your horse. If you're caught in a lightning storm, dismount and lead him away from water, trees, or fences. Try to wait out the storm in a dip, gully, or below a hill.

Finally, know when to stop by listening to your horse. If you plan to tackle a strenuous route or a long ride, estimate his fitness level. Never ride a soft, out-of-shape horse hard, or you could cause permanent damage. An exhausted horse is more likely to stumble or slip.

Your horse might seem fine, but then quit on you. Figure out the reason why he refuses to go up a hill, or spins and tries to head downhill. He could be in pain, in his back or legs.

In some situations, you might need to dismount and lead your horse to safety. Or, up a steep grade, take the burden off his back by "tailing," following him while you grasp his tail so he pulls you up the hill.

When you dismount or mount on the trail, always use the uphill side. The broke horse should not mind your using the off side, and sometimes off side is the only side.

Gear for the Short Ride

When you plan an expedition, specialized equipment can add to your comfort and the comfort of your horse. On a short, casual trail ride, you'll carry only what you need. Plan your equipment according to the climate and length of the ride. A brief tour with no stops can mean simply the same tack you use in the arena — saddle, bareback pad, or even bareback.

"Day packs" can stash small items you'd need on a short ride. You can use a saddle pad or

Riding on the Road

When you venture out, you won't always ride in remote areas. You may even find that most of your trail riding requires you to use roads designed for motor vehicles. Reaching the peace of "unimproved" roadways might mean a half hour's ride beside a busy thoroughfare.

As you ride on or alongside roads, you will realize that the public sees your horse as an unusual, nostalgic form of transportation. You must ride defensively, ready to cope with unexpected events.

First, observe all state and local traffic laws that apply to equestrians. Like other travelers, you have certain rights on public roads. Some states give equestrians the right of way, or they require you to ride on the right, with traffic. All expect you to obey regulatory signs and signals. Ignoring laws endangers you and your horse, and you're not exempt from receiving a traffic citation. This includes riding a horse while intoxicated.

Probably most drivers are unaware of the laws regarding equestrian traffic. On roadways, keep your horse as far from the pavement as possible. Just seeing a horse makes some drivers act silly. Hopefully you will never encounter one who purposely honks to see your horse jump, but these clowns do exist. Anticipate traffic hazards that might impede your progress. Even if you know your horse wouldn't be bothered by a narrow traffic lane, you would obstruct motorized traffic. Try to avoid roads under construction, major bridges, and commuters' favorite shortcuts.

Besides staying alert for motorized traffic, watch out for other forms of transport. Keep a safe distance from bicyclists and skateboarders. Respect pedestrians you encounter along the roadway.

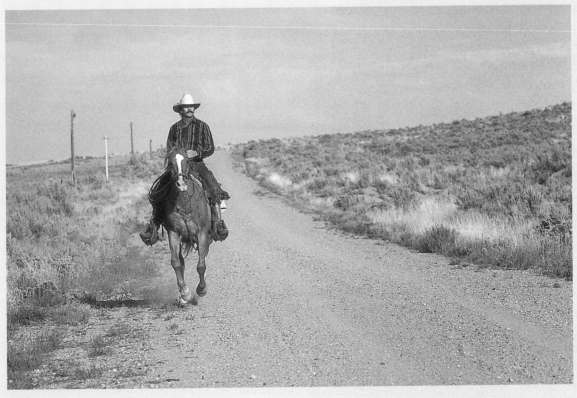

When riding on the road, stay to the far right.

bareback pad with built-in pockets on the back, stationed behind your thighs for a wallet, sunglasses, or camera. Or, wear a close-fitting fanny pack.

You can increase the comfort of any type of saddle with the addition of a seat saver. This fleece pad is shaped to fit over the seat and cantle, providing extra cushion between your seat bones and

Saddlebags are a good choice for carrying a variety of items you may need on the trail.

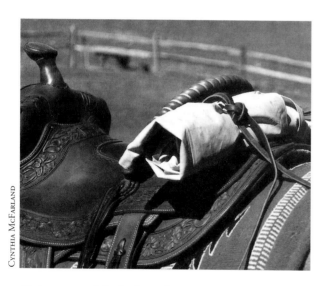

To be prepared for bad weather, you can tie a rolled-up rain slicker behind the cantle using the saddle strings.

Minimal Trail Equipment

You Need This	List of Items	Check for
Horse		In good condition
		Shoes secure
Tack	Saddle	In good repair
	Bridle	Adjusted correctly
	Halter and lead rope	
	Extra leather strap or shoelace	
Personal items	Bag to carry gear	
	First aid kit	
	Hoof pick	
	Camera	
	Whistle	
	Watch	
	Compass and topographic map	
	Sharp pocket knife	
Clothing	Hat	
	Boots	
	Outerwear	

cold, hard leather. A strap underneath the seat holds it securely in place.

Some trail riders like the extra security of tapaderos, or hooded stirrups. On a long ride, these help you maintain your foot position without concentration.

In mountainous terrain, outfit your horse in a comfortable breast collar, strap, or breastplate to prevent the saddle from sliding back. Avoid adding a tiedown, which can hinder the horse's balance. In deep water, a tiedown can even cause a swimming horse to drown.

On a trip lasting several hours with stops along the way, you should bring a halter and lead rope. The easiest way to carry it is to bridle the horse over

The Wide Open Spaces

Ride only where horses are allowed. On some public lands, you may need to buy a permit to ride the trails. If you plan to cross private property, observe property owners' posted signs. Don't assume that a "No Trespassing" sign applies only to vehicles. Always close any gates you open, and be sure you have latched the gate securely.

Farmlands offer unpaved roads for trotting and galloping. Be courteous by skirting the grower's fields. Do not allow your horse to damage any crops, terrain, or equipment. Don't cross irrigation ditches or pipes, as one misstep can block the water flow.

Riding away from traffic gives you a sense of freedom. It also brings you into competition with other users of open space. You and your horse must share paths with hikers, mountain bikes, all-terrain vehicles, off-road motorcycles, 4-wheel drivers, or even skiers.

Rarely will you confront all these hobbyists on the same trail. And, yes, you can co-exist with fellow pleasure-seekers. Many drivers of off-road vehicles will courteously slow down, pull aside, or even stop to allow you to pass.

Again, ride defensively by expecting to deal with varied responses to your presence. Thank the polite drivers, and stay away from the rude ones.

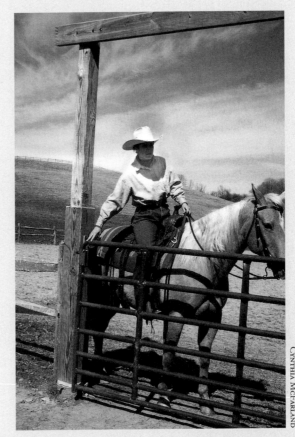

Always close any gates you open, and be sure you have latched the gate securely.

Maybe you're fortunate to have access to bridle trails, dedicated only to equestrian use. Here you'll confront only other riders. Follow the same guidelines you would in a riding ring, keeping a safe distance between horses and alerting riders as you pass at a faster gait. If you pass an oncoming horse, stay to the right as you would when driving a car.

the halter, tying the lead rope loosely around the neck. Or, use a combination halter-bridle.

Tie the horse to a tree short and high, with a quick release knot. You might loosen the cinch during the break, but remind yourself by hanging the near stirrup over the horn.

When you dismount, it's safer to control the horse with a lead rope than the bridle reins. Even if you don't plan to tie him along the way, a halter makes it possible for you to remove the bridle and allow him to munch grass while you relax, holding the rope.

Behind your cantle, you can tie a rolled-up slicker with the saddle strings. A cantle bag or pommel bag can hold a water bottle, day's lunch, hoof pick, first aid kit, camera, and jacket. Tie it behind the cantle by threading the saddle strings through the metal D rings attached to each end of the bag. Be sure to stow any litter in your bag, and pack it back to the barn.

To carry more items, saddlebags are the traditional choice. You can use the traditional style of two large bags connected by a wide yoke, which lies across the rear skirts of the saddle. The bags rest behind your thighs and fasten onto the saddle and rear cinch.

One design, called the "packing" saddlebag, combines the cantle pouch and the gusseted bags. Here a zippered pouch is added onto the yoke.

Whatever bag you choose, don't overload it so the weight irritates your horse. Balance on both sides the weight of items you pack.

Specialized containers are shaped to fasten single items to the saddle. You can find cases designed to carry pliers, wire cutters, a hoof pick, or a camera. A hoof pick case might strap around the flank cinch, and a padded camera bag can rest against the saddle's swells.

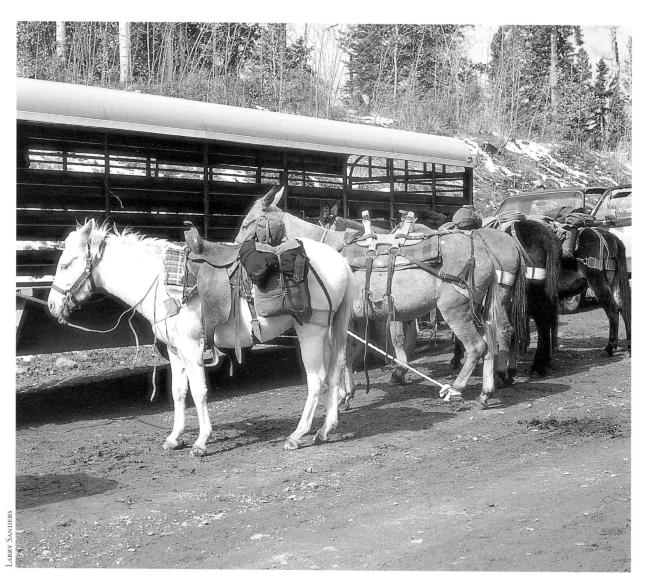

LARRY SANDERS

Certain manufacturers design large, sturdy bags that attach to the saddle and have a crupper to prevent bouncing. Such bags can carry your gear yet still distribute weight evenly. Compression straps keep the load in place. For a longer trip, you can outfit your pack animal with a pack saddle — a combination of harness and saddle tree that allows the most secure arrangement of the greatest load of gear. The mule at the far left is outfitted with pack bags. The mule to his right is outfitted with a pack saddle.

Carry food and drink in functional cases. Choose the old reliable canteen, or a plastic water bottle, which can strap onto another bag.

If you tote a rifle while hunting on horseback, you'll probably carry it in a scabbard. This leather case straps to the rear cinch ring and latigo of the front cinch, to hold the gun at a diagonal angle. Whenever you cross a stream, turn the scabbard to face straight up to protect the gun from water.

When you travel in the high country, even for just a day, dress for changes in weather. Backpackers know to avoid cotton, because wet cotton won't wick water away from your skin. Your body temperature can drop rapidly. Choose synthetic fabrics for inner and outer layers. Gaiters can protect your legs, because jeans can get soaked in a sudden rainstorm. Carry a lightweight, waterproof slicker, to direct water off you and your saddle.

Outfitting Longer Trips

For overnights you can carry camping gear on your saddle horse. By toting your complete outfit on one animal, you reduce the impact on the wilderness environment. Instead of destroying a campsite, you preserve it through limiting yourself to one animal per camper. You also avoid the hassle of securing gear on a packhorse and the constant distraction of worrying about leading him over rough trails.

For this type of packing, choose specialized equipment that applies backpacking technology. Certain manufacturers design large, sturdy bags that attach to saddle and crupper and do not bounce. Such bags can carry your clothing, camping gear, cooking utensils, and dehydrated food, yet still distribute weight evenly. Compression straps keep the load in place.

Whenever you plan to add extra weight onto a horse, practice riding or leading him with all equipment loaded before the trip. This will allow the animal to become used to any unusual shifting, and you can be sure you've fastened all items securely.

By adopting the backpacker's ethic, you'll tread lightly and treat the wilderness with care.

Overnight Equipment	
Horse	Horseshoe repair items or Easyboot Hobbles, overhead picket line equipped with tree saver straps, or picket stake and rope (only if horse is accustomed) Nosebag Horse brush and sponge Antiseptic powder Insect repellent
Backpacker's camping gear	Dehydrated food, utensils, stove, water, matches, flashlight

Proponents of low-impact horse camping find that they can enjoy the peaceful isolation of the back country and leave minimal trace of their travels.

If you do choose to load extra gear onto a pack animal, use a horse, mule, burro, or llama. The pack animal hauls its load in large bags or canvas-wrapped packs (known as "manties"), usually one on each side of its back.

You could substitute canvas saddle panniers. These look like oversized saddle bags, with a wide strap that fits over a Western saddle. A front and a rear cinch fasten over the saddle's regular cinches, and a web breeching strap keeps the panniers from shifting. Avoid overloading your animal. Some horses will only be able to handle a total burden of 100 pounds — 30 pounds in each pannier hung on a 40-pound saddle.

To pack in for a longer time, you'll outfit your beast of burden with a pack saddle. This combination of harness and saddle tree allows the most secure arrangement of the greatest load of gear.

The most common types of pack saddle are the Decker and sawbuck. The Decker is easier to pack. You wrap each portion of the load in a manty and strap a manty on each side of the saddle. The load ties to the Decker's D rings.

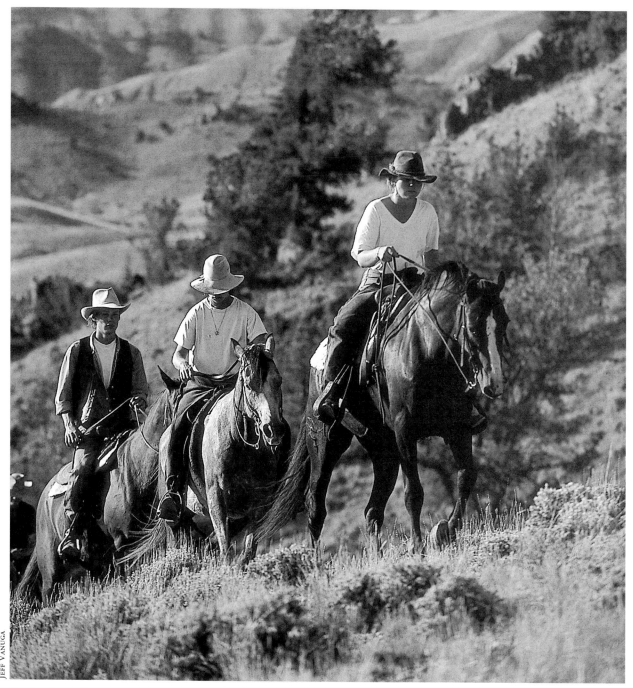

Trail riding allows you to enjoy the scenery of the back country.

On the traditional sawbuck, you tie the load to two pairs of wooden cross pieces. Both types of pack saddles cinch down with a front cinch (the sawbuck adds a rear cinch) over a regular saddle pad or oversized blanket. The saddle stays in place with a breast collar and breeching, pronounced "britchen."

Outfitters rely on the pack saddle and harness to be in top condition. They depend upon pack animals to transport gear during the expedition.

Horse packing is an art, best learned from an expert. Sloppy packs can cause problems ranging from a minor gall to a major disaster on the trail.

Organized Group Rides

Riding with a group, you'll travel 10 to 25 miles a day. The ride can go from one point to another, or form a circular loop back to the starting point. If you start from a ranch or base camp, you can take different excursions each day. Rides can be casual or fancy. You might set up a rustic camp in the wilderness, or you can enjoy catered meals at an elaborate tent city with all the comforts of home.

Be sure your horse is well shod and in shape for the ride. You don't want to hold others up or cause your horse to suffer an injury or loss of a shoe. The ride description should include the type of terrain and the distance, and some rides require health certificates for the horse.

Whether you'll ride for a day or a week, follow the rules of ride officials. The trail boss is the captain of the ride, and his word is law. He knows the route and has permission of landowners, or he's made reservations when you travel across public lands. All riders must remain behind the boss when on the trail, and ahead of the drag riders who bring up the rear of the column of horses.

On a typical ride, the boss leads you out in the morning. Have your horse ready to go before the announced start time. Some rides meet a water truck at designated stops along the trail, so you can offer your horse water (and enjoy a soft drink or beer). You may carry your own lunch or meet the lunch truck at the noon stop.

On a group ride, you'll enjoy scenery of the back country. You'll enjoy wildlife in pine forests, marvel at the desert in bloom, follow historic trails, or see the fall colors. Remember that riders share public lands with other pleasure-seekers, so minimize your horse's impact on the wilderness. Hooves do cause erosion, so always stay on the marked trail and never cut across switchbacks.

Consider your fellow riders and be a good citizen. Stay up with the column of riders. Don't "barge or charge" in the group, and keep the pace set by the trail boss. If you need to stop, move to the side of the trail.

When going through a gate or crossing an obstacle such as a stream, the first riders should walk slowly to maintain an even pace. After crossing, the trail boss should halt the group until everyone arrives on the opposite side (and the last drag rider closes the gate). The horses at the end won't have to trot to catch up with those near the front.

On an overnight ride, the trail boss leads you into camp in late afternoon. You'll unsaddle and

Trail Safety

When you saddle up for the trail, examine your tack on both sides of the horse. Secure your cinch before you start, and check it again about 30 minutes into the ride.

Riding on the trail is an adventure. Keep it fun by riding on safe ground. Avoid glass, cans, holes, or loose wire. Keep a distance between your horse and any possible hazards, such as other animals, a cliff or drop-off, wire fence, or narrow path.

On a group ride, courtesy makes the ride more pleasant and safe. Before you start, wait till everyone is mounted and then walk as a group. If anyone has to stop on the trail, everyone should halt. Horses don't like to be left behind.

Ride only as fast as the least experienced rider can handle. If you see glass on the trail, warn riders behind you with, "Beware glass." Never gallop past another rider — pass no faster than at a trot and call out "Passing." When someone passes, control your horse by angling its head toward the other animal.

care for your horse, letting him rest before offering water and feed. Organized rides will haul feed to the camp, along with your camping gear. Tie your horse to the picket line or to a tree. Station him a safe distance from others, and tie him securely so he won't get loose in the middle of the night.

Resort or Guest Ranch

A resort or guest ranch usually hosts short, all-day, and possibly overnight rides. During your stay, you'll ride a horse assigned to you by the wrangler or outfitter. The horse will be fully equipped, so your dress is your only concern. Overnight rides provide all camping gear, along with a cook and packer.

These rides attract all levels of "city slickers." The wrangler or trail guide might consider his job babysitting, but he wants to make sure you ride safely and enjoy the trip.

On a guest ranch, you may start with riding lessons in the corral. The wrangler might ask you about your riding background, or just assign you a horse and watch you meet the animal. He'll know how much you know about horses by the way you approach the horse, so don't overestimate your horsemanship or you might end up looking like a real tenderfoot.

You may choose a ride with a specific focus, such as one led by a naturalist. Or you might experience the excitement of a cattle drive, where you ride alongside working cowboys. After a long day pushing steers to new pasture, you'll relish supper served from the chuckwagon.

JEFF VANUGA

8

Trail Riding Competitions

Organized distance rides combine the fun of group riding with the challenge of competition. You ride with a goal in mind, and you measure your performance against fellow riders.

Distance riding demands discipline. Through weeks and even months of practice, you condition your horse or mule to a high state of fitness. You don't need a fancy mount to excel in this sport. He has to meet one basic requirement — to cover ground efficiently.

If you like camping and the out-of-doors, distance riding adds the thrill of a contest. If you want to compete but don't like the pressure of the show ring, trail riding provides an ideal equestrian sport. While you prove your ability against other riders, you'll also gain the satisfaction of going "down trail."

Whatever distance they travel, distance riders show "grit," or the heart to continue. You're on the move continuously with the clock ticking, and you cover a range of territory. You aim to ride every

mile, and you and your equine companion become partners who respect and understand each other.

You can participate in various types of rides, with challenges from a few miles to a hundred. In each event, you ride a measured course, marked with signs such as flags or ribbons, from start to finish. Men and women compete equally.

Distance riding differs from other horse sports because the horse's welfare comes first. You prepare your horse by conditioning it for the course. Veterinarians monitor the sport at checkpoints. The ride veterinarian advises you on your horse's physical well-being, and this official can pull you from the contest if your horse displays signs of stress.

The vet analyzes him in four categories: *systemic, locomotor, attitude,* and *lesions.* She evaluates his system by his recovery rate, or how quickly his pulse and respiration (P & R) return to normal. If she judges your horse as exhausted or deyhdrated, you're out.

Type	Goal	Duration	Association
COMPETITIVE TRAIL	To ride a marked trail within a set time period. Judges score horse on time, distance, and stress, and rider on trail equitation and horse care.	2 days 40–60 miles total	North American Trail Riding Conference
ENDURANCE	To complete a marathon in a fast time, while maintaining the horse's well-being	1–3 days 50–100 miles a day 25–35 miles for Limited Distance rides	American Endurance Ride Conference 600 rides a year
RIDE AND TIE	To complete a marathon in a fast time, with two people sharing the same horse. One runs while the other rides.	1 day 6–40 miles	Ride and Tie Association

In distance riding, you and your equine companion become partners who respect and understand each other.

She watches him move, to see if he's "ouchy" or lame. She checks for sole bruises and signs of muscle fatigue. She considers his willingness to keep going, and she checks for any sores caused by your tack or trail injuries.

The Distance-Riding Horseman

All events challenge you in four ways: your animal's physical fitness, his mental attitude, your physical condition, and your strategy in completing the course. Strategy means you plan ahead to meet the event's requirements. You control certain elements, such as conditioning your horse, analyzing the trail, and determining the pace you'll maintain over every mile of the course.

You train your horse to accept the obstacles he's likely to meet on this particular trail. For a level trail on dirt roads, practice in familiar territory. If the course starts on a ski hill, find a mountain trail or steep hill as your training track.

The challenge arises from those factors you can't control — the terrain, the weather conditions, and your competitors. You condition your animal to withstand the stresses he'll undergo, and get yourself in shape to stay alert before, during, and after the ride.

What's His P & R?

During your training and competition, your horse's pulse and respiration, or P & R, indicate his well-being. A normal horse at rest has a pulse of 32 to 44, and a respiration of 40 breaths per minute. As he exercises at walk and trot, uphill and downhill, his heart beats faster and he breathes faster. When you slow down and eventually stop, his P & R slow down. At rest, they recover to normal.

The rate of recovery is an important systemic factor, but you don't need a degree in veterinary medicine to calculate it. To measure your horse's P & R, you count the heartbeats and breaths. You can feel the pulse in several places:

- ✯ Inside the jawbone
- ✯ Behind the nearside elbow
- ✯ At the underside of the tail, about four inches down
- ✯ Underneath the fetlock, at the back of the pastern

Veteran riders use a stethoscope and wristwatch. You'll stand by his near side, wearing

To measure your horse's P & R, you can feel the pulse in several places — inside the jawbone, behind the nearside elbow, the underside of the tail, and under the fetlock, at the back of the pastern.

Capillary refill time is checked by pressing the thumb on the gums, then timing the return of a normal pink color.

the scope, and gently place the concave bell side on the skin behind his elbow. Count the beats for 15 seconds, and multiply by four.

For the respiration, count the number of breaths for 15 seconds. Count the number of times the horse exhales, watching the ribs or flank. Or, use your stethoscope on the underside of the neck, about eight inches below the throatlatch.

Learn your horse's normal P & R, at rest and during various stages of exercise. This preparation will help you keep your horse in good shape as you complete a distance ride.

Ride veterinarians also check capillary refill time to evaluate the horse's hydration. You can easily check this by pressing firmly for a moment on the gum above the front incisors. Release the pressure and count the seconds till the white portion resumes its normal pink color. A refill time of 2 seconds is ideal; longer than 3½ seconds may indicate low blood pressure.

You'll also learn the most important aspect of distance riding — how to pace yourself so you complete the ride in good shape. On the trail, a horseman thinks for the animal — she knows her animal's abilities and knows when to ride conservatively. She doesn't push too much on first rides, because the horse could resent the pressure. When she senses the horse is in pain, she retires from the ride rather than stress the animal unduly.

Your form influences the horse's comfort and your enjoyment. You sit straight in the saddle, adjusting your upper body angle to help him over the terrain. You never sit crooked or sloppily, as your weight influences his efficiency. Dead weight or uneven pressure inhibits his movement and can result in back injuries.

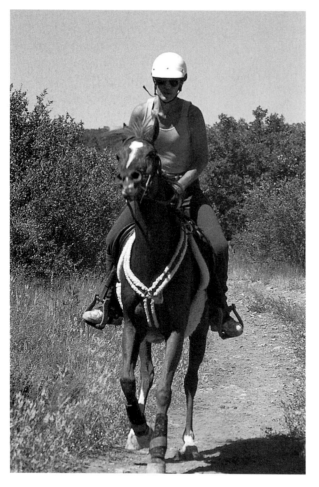

Your form influences the horse's comfort. Sit straight in the saddle, adjusting your upper body angle to help him over the terrain.

Ride on light contact, and at even paces. Most riders use trot and walk, with infrequent breaks of loping. The trot requires less energy and covers ground most efficiently. Over good ground, a horse will trot 10 to 12 miles per hour. You might choose to lope to make up time and vary the gait.

In the trot, keep your weight off the horse's back. Either stand in the two-point position, or post as a break from standing in the stirrups.

During the ride, you care for your horse. You keep him hydrated by offering water available at checkpoints. You also carry water with you, so you can offer it to him, drink it yourself, or cool him off by dousing him.

When you join these events, you'll realize that the dedicated riders aim to bring their horses to the finish in better shape than when they left the starting line. Your goal should be to work your horse hard on the trail, and the next day see him bounce back from stress without displaying any adverse effects. Just like the horses of the early West, he's ready for another round.

Other horsemen often label distance riders as "mavericks." The sport can become an obsession, because you must focus on so many aspects of horsemanship — health, biomechanics, tack, and psychology. To succeed, you must know your horse so well that you immediately recognize any unusual behavior and discover the reason.

Distance riders share a unique support system. You may not always ride in a group, but most competitors willingly offer help to one another on the trail.

Tack for Distance Riding

If you plan to concentrate on distance riding, consider switching to a lightweight endurance saddle. Weighing 20 pounds or less, the endurance saddle can resemble a barrel racing model, without a horn.

Back soreness plagues endurance horses, and a well-fitted saddle is crucial to keeping the horse going through the season. A few American saddlemakers build models designed to eliminate undue pressure on the horse's back and withers. Bars should avoid any edge pressure. The tree and rigging are constructed to distribute weight evenly and to avoid interference with the action of the shoulder blades. One unique brand has hinged bars that adjust to the shape of the horse's back as the horse's muscles develop.

For rider comfort, the seat is narrow and the stirrups are hung directly under your center of gravity. Look for a seat that keeps your back straight so you sit in a balanced position on long rides. If you suffer from back pain, the right seat can alleviate much agony.

The saddle should have metal rings so you can attach a breastplate and an optional crupper. You'll also strap on a cantle bag and two water bottle carriers. Some riders tie a sponge or scoop onto the saddle, for cooling the horse with water.

The McClellan saddle, made famous as the official saddle of the U.S. Cavalry, is a favorite with many trail riders. It was designed for extended travel, so the saddle favors the horse's comfort. Although some people suffer from the saddle's seat, fans of the McClellan saddle claim it is the ideal choice.

Many distance riders use some style of seat saver, such as a sheepskin, on top of the saddle. The padding adds comfort on those long miles. Under the saddle, use a saddle pad that avoids any pressure points. Several manufacturers offer specialty pads that transmit pressure uniformly over a broad area of the horse's back. These absorb shock, and some materials mold to the ever-changing shape of the horse in motion. A pad also must wick moisture

Choose specially designed distance riding tack for your own and your horse's comfort.

from the horse's coat. Natural fabrics like wool or wool felt let the skin breathe and remain cool.

Help keep your saddle in place on inclines with a breast collar. A Y-shaped collar keeps the saddle from shifting sideways or backward, and it avoids rubbing the shoulder muscles. You might need a crupper on a mule or a horse with low withers. This tack will keep the saddle from sliding forward when you walk down a steep hill.

Look for lightweight stirrups that will support your feet on the long miles. Stirrups should absorb shock and have wide treads for comfort.

Many distance riders prefer a bitless bridle, such as a hackamore or even a halter (usually with a bit attached). The horse can eat or drink more comfortably on the trail, especially during longer rides when it's crucial to keep his system operating at full capacity.

Be sure to train in the same gear you'll use during the ride. Try out new equipment at home to confirm it fits the horse and stays in place. A new saddle blanket can be so slick it slides off, even with the saddle cinched.

Wear lightweight, comfortable clothing appropriate for the weather conditions. Many distance riders wear spandex riding tights. Faux suede insets keep your leg secure against the saddle. Padded tights add cushioning at crotch and knee. Choose outerwear of synthetic fabrics like microfiber or polar fleece, depending on the climate. Fabric should wick moisture away from your body so you don't overheat or become chilled.

You might choose to wear riding shoes rather than boots, so you can ride and run in your footwear. Riding shoes support and protect the an-

Assistants take pulse and respiration counts at planned and unplanned stops throughout the ride.

	Open Division	Novice	Competitive Pleasure
RIDE TYPES	B (1 day) A (2 days) AA (3 days)	B (1 day) A (2 days)	B (1 day) A (2 days)
RIDER CLASSES	Heavyweight (190 lbs & over) Lightweight (100–189 lbs) Junior (no weight limit)	Heavyweight (190 lbs & over) Lightweight (100–189 lbs) Junior (no weight limit)	Only 1 rider class (no weight limit)

kle from rubbing against the stirrup leather. Ribbed soles help you keep your foot in position.

Be sure to wear protective headgear. Equestrian helmets are accepted in this sport, with visors to shade your head from the sun. Junior riders must wear an ASTM/SEI-approved helmet in order to compete in North American Trail Riding Conference (NATRC) competitions.

Competitive Trail Riding

In NATRC competition, all horses complete an identical trail in the same length of time. Officials judge the horse's soundness, condition, and manners, along with your horsemanship. In NATRC, the combined weight of rider and tack determines your weight class.

To organize and manage the ride involves a ride chairman and a trailmaster. The trailmaster determines the trail, within the guidelines set by NATRC. She uses a topographic map to track the mileage and timing of the trail. Open and Novice divisions may use the same trail, with different times, lengths of hill climbs, and additional mileage for the Open riders.

The goal is to determine the best trail horses, the animals that can cover the course with the least stress. During a ride, competitors must observe rules about caring for their horses. Rules prohibit treatments with

medications or using any leg wraps or boots. Supplements of salt, electrolytes, vitamins, feed, and water are permissible by use of oral syringe. In addition, a rider is allowed to use fly spray or apply water.

NATRC also limits the type of horseshoes by width and thickness. You may use only rim pads. In an emergency, you may use an Easyboot as temporary hoof protection.

A ride has at least two judges, who score horse and rider. The veterinary judge rates the horse for condition (40%), soundness (45%), and trail ability/manners (15%). The horsemanship judge evaluates the rider for grooming (20%), trail equitation (50%), and trail care (30%).

Under current rules, horse and rider start with 100 points each. Judges deduct penalties for deviations from the ideal. In each division, the winning horse completes the ride with the most points for the best condition. The winning rider is the superior horseman, earning the most points.

Judges examine each animal before the ride and each ride morning, noting his condition on a judging card. To arrive at a baseline, they evaluate health, soundness, and way of going, and they note marks and blemishes.

Officials observe horses throughout the ride, at planned and unplanned stops. P & R workers take pulse and respiration counts at the stops. NATRC requires two P & R checks per day, although some rides or divisions of rides have three or four. After the ride, the horse is checked by a vet that evening and again the next morning.

On an NATRC ride, your goal is to conquer the trail environment and to bring your mount to the finish line safe and sound. You prove yourself a responsible horseman when you keep the horse relaxed and comfortable. To the dedicated rider, awards rank secondary to this goal.

The Competitive Ride

At the ride, you'll receive a map of the trail showing turns, elevations, mileage, and water stops. You leave the starting point individually, usually at a 30-second interval after the previous rider.

You'll set your watch at a zero point, such as 12:00, when you start. Using the map, you see the time you should arrive at the first designated P & R check. If this is an hour and 20 minutes and measures 4.6 miles, you figure out how fast to travel. The map lists the elevations on the route, so you know when to walk and when to trot.

"We time the trail by walking rocks and trotting the good terrain," NATRC National Champion Audrey Taylor has explained. "Open riders trot down some easy hills, and up some slants. Novice riders walk most everything, except they trot good terrain."

Plan your strategy according to the distance, terrain, and weather conditions. You'll use your discretion to ride at your own pace, watching the time so you know what speed to adopt during various stages of the trail. You must remain in the saddle during the ride, not walk or run beside your horse or tail it.

NATRC rules specify that you arrive at designated checkpoints within a 30-minute time frame. You can come in 15 minutes before or after the specific time. Arriving any earlier or later costs you penalty points, one for each minute.

"You have to work as a team," says Taylor. "That's my favorite thing about this sport. If you don't, then you'll be too early, or too late. After a while, the horse gets to know when you would ask for a trot, and when you'd want to walk."

Your horse figures out the pace and learns how to conserve his energy. He tells you how he feels by his energy level, and he tells you when he's ready to move out. If he says, "Let's trot," he's telling you he feels good. "Let's lope" could mean he's tired of trotting and his muscles could use a change. Or if you communicate, "Do you feel like trotting?" you gauge his energy level by his response. He may grudgingly change gait, which tells you he's getting tired.

At a vet check, officials examine the horse to see if he meets the P & R parameters. When you arrive at the check, a timer checks you in, with your check time recorded at 10 minutes ahead. Your horse has that time period to recover.

When the 10 minutes are up, the vet will take the P & R for 15 seconds. Your horse should show a pulse of 12, and a respiration of 6. You earn one point penalty for each count over the parameter.

Depending on the heat, the vet may raise the P & R to a higher measurement. If the parameter is a pulse of 16 and your horse's is higher, the vet will "hold" him for another 10 minutes and then recheck. You have to wait those 10 minutes, with the time added to your end ride time.

With temperature, terrain, and condition affecting P & R, you also concern yourself with how your horse moves during the ride. For example, if he bangs his leg on a rock, you should notice the unusual movement.

You'd dismount, soak your sponge or bandana from your water bottle, and soak the leg to cool it. (If you're out of water, briskly rub the leg.) The temporary pain will cause his pulse to rise, but it should slow as you treat the area.

Competitive trail riding is the only distance riding that includes horsemanship judging. The horsemanship judge observes how you handle your horse, both on the ground and in the saddle. You'll also receive scores for how you groom the horse, how you control him in hand, and your tack. For the veterinary examinations, hold the reins or lead rope while standing on the same side as the vet. Keep your horse under control, because his manners count toward his score and yours.

Stay on the Trail

A major hazard in distance riding is getting lost. In almost every ride, somebody ignores the map or misses the markers. This rider has to backtrack, losing time or points.

Ride officials post ribbons of surveyor's tape to mark the trail. Usually they'll "ribbon" the course with the ribbons on the right, tied high on tree limbs. Three ribbons means a turn is coming up, and next will be three more ribbons marking the actual turn. For a left turn, you'd see two ribbons on the right, and one on the left.

To follow the route, study your map and watch for the ribbons, or hoofprints of earlier riders. If you get lost, go back to the last ribbon you saw.

If you get lost, blame yourself for failing to pay attention. Don't blindly follow a rider or group ahead of you, because someone else could easily make the mistake first and you could succumb to their error.

If you're tired, you might miss a marker and go down the wrong trail. If you do find yourself lost and your horse hasn't learned where "home" is, wait for the drag riders to find you. Carry a whistle for such a circumstance, and blow it at intervals to broadcast your location.

Judges test your trail skills with obstacles. You might have to walk or sidepass over a log, back your horse (always look first to see if it's safe), or maneuver around rocks. Depending on the terrain, other tests could involve crossing water, stepping down a steep, winding path, or dismounting and mounting on the off side. Judges look for a safe, calm trail horse and a smart rider who thinks through the obstacle.

As you approach the end of the ride, you must maintain forward motion for the last two miles. Rules prohibit you from stopping or dismounting along this final segment of the trail.

Base Camp

On distance rides, riders and their horses live at base camp. Usually in a meadow or valley, the campsite resembles a recreational vehicle parking lot. But you don't need a fancy motor home, because you can bunk down in the back of a pickup or on the ground.

In camp, you care for your horse after the day's ride. On some rides, camp also serves as the lunch stop.

Your horse stays tied to the trailer, to an overhead picket line, or in a portable corral. He needs to relax in camp. The freedom of a corral encourages him to stretch out, and as soon as you unsaddle and leave him alone, he's likely to urinate.

Because you concentrate on caring for your horse and planning for (or recovering from) the ride, you probably won't spend much time "camping." These are family sports, and your family or friends come along to enjoy the outdoor life (and take care of the housekeeping while you do the horsekeeping).

In camp, you'll make friends with your fellow competitors. Distance riders share a camaraderie in their love for horses and their obsession with the sport. Most old hands enjoy sharing experiences and opinions, so you can ask lots of questions. Some rides will distribute name tags designating novice and open riders, so you know whom to ask. The experts will also freely offer advice, so maintain an open mind and thank them for their help.

Your horse care in camp becomes part of your horsemanship score in competitive trail riding. Judges can score you on how you feed, water, and tie your horse. NATRC rules govern stabling and

Judges will score you on how you feed, water, and tie your horse in camp. If the camp doesn't have separate corrals, every rider has to tie her horse to a stationary object (usually the horse trailer).

limit the hours of horse care. To keep the competition fair, all riders must secure their horses in the same way. If the camp doesn't have separate corrals, every rider has to tie her horse to a stationary object (usually the horse trailer).

Endurance Riding

Among all equestrian sports, this discipline places the most demanding test upon horse and rider. The horse's physical and mental capacities affect how well he can cover ground cross-country, within a specified time period. Endurance riding is the only international sport open to riders who choose Western style. The U.S. Equestrian Team added endurance riding in 1993.

Because the event originated in North America, riders from the United States have dominated the World Championships. Becky Hart and her Arabian "Rio" have won this title three times.

Inspired by frontier treks, endurance riding reflects the Western heritage. Rides often follow pioneers' trails, yet today's riders apply scientific data to maximize the horse's travel and minimize the stress.

This marathon involves skill and stamina. The American Endurance Ride Conference (AERC) has a motto: "To finish is to win." Riders follow another guideline: "The trail is your competition." To succeed, riders focus on the goal of completing the ride within the specified maximum time. Competition does drive some riders, who concentrate on the race aspect to finish with the forerunners.

As a novice, your goal is to complete the ride. Plan your strategy accordingly, and begin your endurance career with a training ride. Riding competitive trail can teach you horse care that you'd apply to endurance riding.

AERC sanctions rides of varying distances. For beginners, AERC sanctions the Limited Distance ride of 25 to 35 miles. This is held in conjunction with a regular AERC ride.

The ride strategy resembles that of competitive trail riding. The map marks every designated rest stop, or check, set at regular intervals. Study the map to calculate your speed to each check, so you can plan your rate of travel. On your first rides, you'll aim for an average speed of four to six miles per hour.

Your pit crew will meet you at each check. At least one, preferably two or more, helpers will assist you in caring for your horse. Experienced riders may choose to ride solo, without a crew to assist.

During this break, you'll help your horse to recover his pulse to 68 or below. You'll check his shoes, offer feed and water, and dose him with electrolytes to restore his hydration. After removing the tack, you'll sponge him on his neck and legs to reduce the pulse rate. You might drape a soaked towel on his neck, or apply iced leg wraps to reduce any swelling. Many endurance riders use TTEAM techniques to relieve temporary muscular aches.

Each check includes a veterinary examination. The veterinarian determines if your horse can continue the ride safely.

The Endurance Ride

Before you tackle the ride, learn as much as you can about the course. You might ride the entire trail to learn it. Pre-ride the last leg, so your horse learns where home is. This can stimulate his homing instinct on the last miles.

Attend the pre-ride briefing to find out how the trail is marked. Officials will describe specific hazards and explain the veterinary criteria. You can also ask fellow riders about the trail.

AERC has developed rules and guidelines for a standardized format. Strict veterinary controls begin with a pre-ride exam. The veterinarian will determine the horse's starting condition. She checks the cardiovascular system, hydration, gut sounds, and overall health.

All riders usually leave at the same time in a "shotgun" start. Before the start, walk and trot your horse slowly. Take your time when you do travel along the trail, letting the faster horses hurry to the front so you can maintain control over yours.

Riders soon spread out, so you can pace your horse so he doesn't wear himself out. You may decide to ride in a group moving at a comfortable pace, but maintain control if others pass you. Don't let the excitement lure you into trying to keep up with faster riders, whose pace might tire your horse before you realize it. And don't let him decide he has to stay with the group; he should be able to work alone and not waste energy fretting about horses ahead of, or behind, him.

You'll usually ride at the trot. As you near a vet check, walk your horse so his P & R will drop.

You'll come into two types of holds, or time spent in vet checks, that don't count in the total ride time. Timers record your arrival and departure

American Endurance Ride Conference (AERC) Rides

RIDE TYPES			CLASSES	
Ride Mileage	Time	Checks	Senior Division	Junior Division
50 miles	12 hours	4	Lightweight (160 lbs. and below)	All riders under the age of 16
100 miles	24 hours	8	Middleweight (161–210 lbs.)	
150 miles	36 hours	—	Heavyweight (211 lbs. and over)	

times at each check. Some vet checks are mandatory holds, where you stay a set amount of time. You don't have to come into this hold with a low P & R.

Most vet checks have a "gate" into the hold. Before you present your horse for the examination, his pulse must recover to an announced requirement (usually between 72 and 64). The lower his pulse when you near the vet check, the sooner you can pass through the gate into the hold, and the sooner you can resume the ride.

At every check, the veterinarian evaluates metabolic and mechanical indicators. She pulls horses that aren't fit to continue. If you've overridden your horse or pushed him beyond his ability, he won't recover quickly. The vet will check gut sounds and anal tone as indicators of fatigue, along with other signs like inversion (pulse faster than respiration) and panting.

Heidi Caldwell, a rider with 20 years in the sport, was on the pit crew for Teresa Cross at the 1990 World Championships. She explains the use of water at the vet checks. "You must maintain your hydration, so the more water we get in and around these horses when it starts getting warm the more we can keep the jets cooled down. Horses generate a lot of body heat from their working muscles. Their temperature can rise by a number of degrees. So you need to have that extra cooling, and the evaporation of the water helps cool these horses.

"There are certain areas of the body you don't want to put it on when they're working like that. You tend to stay away from the hindquarters and the large muscle masses over the back and the loins. They can cramp up with a heavy dousing of cold water. We usually douse the neck, the shoulders, the legs, and the chest in between the front legs. The rider can use a squeeze water bottle to keep the horse cool while they're moving."

The horse with strength and courage excels in this sport. In a fit horse, the heart rate can increase with exercise to 120 to 200 beats per minute. Within 10 to 15 minutes, that rate should drop dramatically. A horse with a high recovery rate has a pulse that comes down fast.

On the ride, you need to take care of yourself. You can lose 10 pounds on a ride, so keep yourself hydrated. Dunk a bandana in water, and tie it around your neck. Drink a lot of water, before you feel thirsty, and also eat snacks like oranges so you don't get heat exhaustion. If you become woozy and lose your form, it affects the horse.

On a mandatory hold, like an hour lunch break, you and your horse can relax. You may or may not decide to unsaddle. Leaving the saddle on keeps the back muscles warm; removing it cools the muscles. On a longer ride, you might switch to a fresh saddle pad and girth cover, or even a different saddle.

At the completion of the ride, an official will weigh you and your tack. This determines your class in the ride. Your horse undergoes a final vet check, and if he's met all criteria, you've successfully completed the ride.

Famous endurance rides include the World Championships (where riders represent the U.S. Equestrian Team), the Western States Trail Ride (the Tevis Cup), and the Race of Champions. You must qualify to enter the Race of Champions, considered the toughest in the United States. This three-day ride covers 160 miles in the high country.

Ride and Tie

Ride and tie originated in the Old West, where two people occasionally had to share one horse. As a sport, this distance race spreads the challenge across three team members — a horse and two riders. While one person rides, the other walks or runs, so runners and riders alternate on the trail in this unique version of the biathlon.

Most ride and tie events run for 10 to 20 miles. The shortest distance is about 6 miles, with the World Championship race at 40.

In ride and tie, you and your human partner decide who rides the horse what distance. If you start riding, you travel the trail as you would in endurance riding. You pace the trail and read your horse, while considering the ability of your teammate. When you've ridden as far as you think your teammate can run, you halt, dismount, and tie the horse to a tree along the trail. You then continue the course at a walk or jog. The horse waits for your partner to catch up, untie him and mount, and then the two of them follow you. The three of you meet, and you agree who gets the horse for the next segment. (Rules prohibit riding double or one tailing the horse.)

Is ride and tie a horse sport, or a people sport? It places unusual demands on the three athletes who make up the team. You have to be in shape for a cross-country marathon, in addition to handling the horse down trail. You'll spend a major percentage of the race time on foot rather than in the saddle. (Riders and runners must switch a minimum number of times.) The horse has to show both mental willingness and physical fitness. Besides being fit for the distance, he must cope with the stop-and-go conditions of the ride.

Ride and tie contestant Lisa Skyhorse explains: "The horse has to be mentally reasonable. You tie him up and run away from him. Meanwhile, other horses pass him on the trail. It takes a lot of athleticism, too. He either sprints, or he stands still."

The standing still part poses difficulties for many equine athletes. The veteran ride and tie horse knows to take advantage of the rest period during his breaks. A seasoned endurance horse, conditioned to maintain constant motion, might fret and fight the tie rope. If he gets untied, he'll run down the trail with the pack, or travel home to base camp. (He'll probably pass either you or your teammate on the way!) All three of you must cross the finish line together to complete the race, so an equine dropout can disqualify you.

The ride includes vet checks, usually about every 10 miles. A pit crew can assist you at the checks. You and your teammate must exchange the horse at least twice between vet checks. Officials examine horses and mules for P & R, capillary refill, soundness, and abrasions, and they pull animals who don't meet the criteria. After completion, the horse must also pass a post-race examination.

The Ride and Tie Ride

You'll probably compete wearing riding tights or shorts in warm weather. (Protect your legs by sprinkling talcum powder over the saddle during the ride.) Racers wear running shoes.

At the starting line, everyone sets off at once in a shotgun start. In a major race of 120 entries, you'll run with 120 horses and 120 runners. (If you start on foot, you'll be wise to position yourself behind the equine racers at the start.)

Some teams plan ride strategy, aiming for the superior runner to handle the tougher parts of the trail. However, you can't always plan your exact trade-off points. Other riders may have used all the available trees for tying their horses, and you'll have to continue till you find a proper spot. You must tie in a safe location beside the trail, where your partner can spot the horse.

Ride and tiers recommend a special rope, measuring about 3½ feet long with strong clips on each end. You don't actually tie the rope, you wrap it around the tree and snap the clip to the wrap. This quick wrap should hold the horse securely.

If you're in the saddle when you arrive at the first vet check, you must present your horse to officials. Your crew helps you by offering water and snacks, filling your water bottles, and helping the horse recover. The horse can't continue until he passes the veterinary criteria and the runner arrives at the check. You can start running as soon as you're ready. Most vet checks use the "hand tie," where a crew member holds the horse's rope instead of your tying the horse to an object.

When the runner arrives, the horse should have passed the check and should be ready to continue. The runner mounts and follows the course.

As you walk or jog along the trail, you don't know exactly how much time and distance separate you from the horse and rider. You may expect them to overtake you within 15 minutes, but a delay

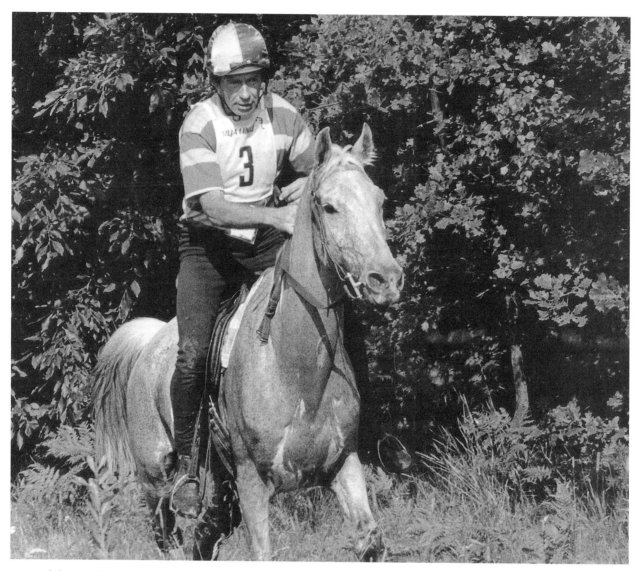

A good distance horse must be mentally and physically conditioned. The best ones are lean, streamlined athletes that are fit but not overly muscled.

could occur if the officials hold the horse. Your crew could ask other riders to tell you what's happening, but you might keep running farther than you had planned.

A top, two-man team averages six miles per hour in ride and tie. They could complete a 28-mile course in 2½ hours. Teams of both genders or two-woman teams usually take longer to complete the ride. You can compete as husband and wife, parent and child, or go for the "Century" category, in which the ages of all three team members add up to at least 100.

The Horse for the Distance

Distance riders look for a certain type of equine athlete. This horse is lean and sinewy, with light muscles of the slow-twitch type. The muscles expand and contract more slowly than those of the fast-twitch type. The horse can dissipate heat faster and endure repeated efforts over a longer duration.

Becky Hart describes her World Champion Arabian, R. O. Grand Sultan: "The thing that makes him a good endurance horse is that mechanically he's put together very well. He's got short cannons, deep heart girth — all the things you look for in a good endurance horse. Along with the conformation, he's got the heart and the desire. He does it because he loves it."

A successful distance horse flows over the trail with no wasted motion. At the walk and trot, he seems to spring forward. He has substantial feet and correct angles on all joints.

NATRC rules require a Novice horse to be at least 48 months of age; an Open horse, 60 months. AERC requires the horse in a Limited Distance ride to be at least 48 months.

The distance riding horse must have a good walk and trot. One that moves slowly, without expending much energy, can frustrate the rider. This animal may maintain low pulse and respiration rates, but other animals will pass it on the trail.

Champions are "lean machines," streamlined athletes that are fit but not overly muscled. The sport tests these horses against a standard of performance, and some breeders have succeeded in producing animals that have the ability for the sport.

Although individuals of any breed can compete and win, Arabian and half-Arabian horses (and mules) dominate distance riding. Originally bred to endure desert treks, these animals consistently outride the more contemporary breeds.

Besides looking like a distance horse, the animal must have the metabolism to handle the test. He can carry weight, yet he converts energy into forward movement. He has a hearty appetite and readily drinks available water. He also shows a "can-do" attitude, with the spirit to keep moving toward the finish line.

A distance prospect benefits from an early life running free in a pasture. A youngster builds bone density through ranging over a large area of uneven terrain. He learns to cope with the elements and handle himself if exposed early to an environment that contains hills, rocks, and running water.

Benefits of Conditioning

To bring your horse to a state of fitness, you apply both science and equestrian art. You focus on your riding goals and prepare your animal to meet the test.

Distance riders develop a variety of approaches to conditioning, but all require consistent work. Through increased physical demands, your animal becomes fit. Heart, lungs, muscles, and mind all must function at full capacity in the equine athlete. Fitness implies well-being, a combination of inherited soundness, proper nutrition, and regular workouts.

Conditioning builds your horse up to his genetic potential. The fit athlete is strong, confident, and injury-free. Through a planned workload, he's ready for competition. His muscles are flexible; they stretch and flex rather than pull and tear.

A conditioning program of higher-energy activity improves the horse's strength, endurance, balance, flexibility, and agility. Through planned exercise, you exert muscles, strengthen the cardiovascular system, and build up the animal's basic structure.

Briefly, increased activity overloads the body's cells. Responding to stress, the cells enlarge. You may not see your horse's muscles grow bigger, but the cells can process and maintain energy for longer periods.

Exercise stimulates the cardiovascular (heart and blood circulation) and respiratory (breathing) systems. Stress requires the heart to pump blood faster through the body, and the lungs to inhale faster, sending energy to all cells. As these systems increase in their efficiency, the horse's pulse and respiration maintain acceptable levels during exercise. Increased stress of time and intensity helps the horse build strong bone, thick cartilage, and strong tendons and ligaments.

Your equine athlete will benefit from increasingly stressful aerobic and anaerobic exercise. Aerobics, also popular in human workouts, develop the cardiovascular system. Fast-paced, steady movement stimulates faster, deeper breathing, which stresses the heart and lungs to

Pony your horse by leading him while you ride another.

supply cells with more oxygen. You elevate the heart rate and hold it up in "cruise control" for several minutes.

Anaerobic exercise stresses the muscles by demanding quick energy. A short sprint or a rapid hill climb are anaerobic workouts, which strengthen muscles already toned by moderate exercise. In competition, you reserve anaerobic work for a sprint to the finish line.

You can condition a horse without riding it, through ponying. Pony your horse by leading him while you ride another. Be sure you can ride with the reins in one hand, and outfit the ponied horse in a stout halter and a long enough lead rope. School the ponied horse to travel close to your right, its head beside your knee. Practice in an enclosed area before you pony a horse on the trail.

A Conditioning Program

Your program begins with a goal, usually the length of the season's first ride. Develop your program gradually, so your horse can adjust to increased stress. Usually, you want him to peak about 10 days before the ride. Then you maintain his condition throughout the riding season.

Always help your horse stretch before a training session, and warm up at the walk. And vary the terrain you cover in your workouts. As NATRC champion Audrey Taylor has said, "You have to build the whole horse." She recommends hill climbs one day, then resting the mountain climbing muscles and trotting hard-packed ground to build bone density.

You might get by with a three-month program for a short competitive trail ride, but training an endurance horse takes longer. Besides building muscles, you strengthen tendons and condition bone.

If you begin with a horse that is out of shape, you might ride him daily for 30 minutes at a walk, then add the trot, for two to four weeks of legging up. Gradually increase the distance and speed during the next few weeks, with more trot and canter work.

Scrutinize your horse constantly during the training period. Be sure the farrier shoes him for distance riding, with pads if you'll be traveling over rocky trails. Watch for signs of excess stress.

Developing a moderately fit horse takes from three to six months of regular exercise of heart, lungs, and muscles. For example, you could start with four to six miles for two weeks, then move up to an eight-mile ride one day. Encourage your horse to develop a ground-covering trot, and use "long trotting" (about 10 miles per hour) as an efficient aerobic exercise. This gait will build up his wind and encourage him to move at a steady rhythm. (If you post, change your diagonals frequently.) Gradually increase the time you trot, and move up to trying 10 to 12 miles one day a week. You'll probably ride the horse five or six days a week to get him in condition. For more than moderate fitness, you must work daily, or six days on, one day off. Check the P & R after a long trot, aiming for him to recover after a 10-minute rest.

Measure training trails so you can calculate your speed. Post mile markers, and move them to different terrain to learn how your speed changes as you move up or down, or across difficult footing.

Conditioning bone takes longer than conditioning muscles and requires low intensity, long duration work. Include this type of exercise in your regular conditioning program. The time required varies according to the horse's condition,

Site	Item	Use
ON THE HORSE	Hoof pick	Pick out the horse's feet
	Easyboot	Apply if horse loses a shoe
	Vet card in plastic bag	Present at vet checks
	1 or 2 water bottles	Drinking and cooling (pour water over the horse's poll as needed)
	Stethoscope	Taking P & R
	Sponge	Cooling horse at water crossing
THE RIDER CARRIES	Wristwatch	Keeps track of riding time
	Fanny pack	Contains rainwear, knife, whistle, flashlight or glow bar, high-energy snacks

age, and your adherence to a daily schedule. Avoid rushing or shortcuts to prevent stressing body or mind.

For a more strenuous ride, increase the mileage and add more stressful anaerobic work, also called "interval training." Usually this would be short sprints at a gallop, either on the flat or up a grade. Mountain trails shorten the time to get a horse fit. For hill climbs, you might start with 200 yards, then work up to a half-mile climb.

By stepping up the duration and speed of workouts, you'd need about 8 weeks to ready a moderately fit horse for a 2-day, 75-mile trail ride. Try a 30-mile test as a conditioning ride.

When the horse is fit, some trainers feel you should work him hard one day, then give him some time off for muscles to rebuild. The fit horse could go on a 20-mile ride every other week. You can probably keep him in shape with about 25 miles a week. This might be through one, two, or three rides a week. You could go 10 to 15 miles on a weekend, with two 5-mile rides during the week. Becky Hart says she keeps her horses in shape by riding 4 to 6 miles three times a week, for 45 to 60 minutes.

Work on your fitness, too. You need to maintain your alertness on the trail so you can guide your horse. Endurance riders spend time on the ground, leading or tailing. In tailing, you help your horse surmount a hill by dismounting and holding on to the horse's tail. Don't pull the tail as he walks up the hill, but let him tow you.

Downhill, you may choose to walk beside your horse. This groundwork demands that you be in shape. You may find yourself jogging alongside during your training sessions, and you can also swim or work out to toughen your legs for those hours of trotting down trail.

Test your conditioning program with a novice competitive ride or a limited distance endurance ride. Besides evaluating your horse's fitness, you'll discover how he adapts to the campsite, the ride officials, the other horses, and unfamiliar terrain.

Competitive Strategies

Distance riding presents a challenge because you must pace your horse to conserve energy as you ride against the trail. Winning strategy begins with training your horse, both on the ground and in the saddle. He has to accept handling from strangers, as he'll undergo veterinary examinations during the event. You may have conditioned your animal to a high level of fitness, but he also must cooperate to allow the ride officials to check his pulse and respiration.

Distance riding tests your horse, so plan how to maximize his strength and fitness. By balancing the effects of distance, terrain, altitude, and weather, you'll know when to "motor out," or push ahead, and when to slack off and ride conservatively.

You need to know how much horse you have left, especially if the hardest part of the trail is in its second half. Here you might save your horse for the tough sections, so he's mentally and physically alert enough to pick his way over tree roots or rocky ground, while still maintaining a good pace.

Your horse will tell you how he feels. If he stumbles once or twice, he may be tiring. If he's breathing hard during a trot, slow down so his respiration rate drops closer to normal.

During training, you should learn what type of trail he prefers. He could thrive on hills but lack speed on the flat. Or if he hates trudging through sand, plan to make up lost time on an earlier or later section of the trail.

In distance riding, you develop a close rapport with your horse. You learn every aspect of his physical state and normal behaviors, and you're attuned to any variation. You can tell when he moves easily, and a slightly different feel could indicate he's sore or fatigued. When your horse moves differently in the mountains, you have to decide if he's suffering from altitude sickness, bored with his job, or simply tired from struggling up hills.

Through pitting yourself against the trail, you learn the limits of your horse's abilities, and you'll discover when he "hits the wall" and has nothing left. You don't want to push him too hard, or he may sulk and not want to leave the base camp.

If he falls on the trail, try to determine what caused the fall. He might have slipped and lost his momentum, or fatigue might have caused him to stumble. Some horses don't seem to care about losing their footing, which endangers both you and them.

Critics challenge distance riding, especially endurance, citing the stress that riders inflict on their animals. However, most contestants do put the horse's welfare first, often above their own. You'll see weary riders who struggle to stay awake, while their horses appear fresh and ready to continue. AERC rules prohibit the use of any drugs during a ride, even forbidding the use of liniment until after the final vet check.

A conditioned endurance horse thrives on his task. He receives better care than most equine athletes, and probably more veterinary attention. With veterinarians monitoring the events, a 100-miler has as many as 10 examinations before, during, and after the ride.

The distance horse proves himself through competition. It may take 1,000 miles for an endurance horse to begin to thrive on competition. The champion develops a will to win. He wants to stay ahead of the pack, and he knows when other horses travel in front of him.

Distance riding also concentrates on trail preservation. Enthusiasts cooperate with government agencies to ensure open space and dedicated trails. Horsemen prove they're responsible users of public lands and aim to conserve natural resources.

Appendixes

THE
WESTERN HORSE

Tack Components

A   Bosal
B   Billet (also called "latigo")
C   Throat latch
D   Horn
E   Pommel
F   Cantle
G   Cinch
H   Flank billet
I   Fender

Anatomy

1   Pastern
2   Gaskin
3   Croup
4   Cannon bones
5   Stifle
6   Knee
7   Shoulder
8   Poll
9   Crest
10 Point of hock
11 Fetlock

Parts of the Hoof

Coronary band

Hoof

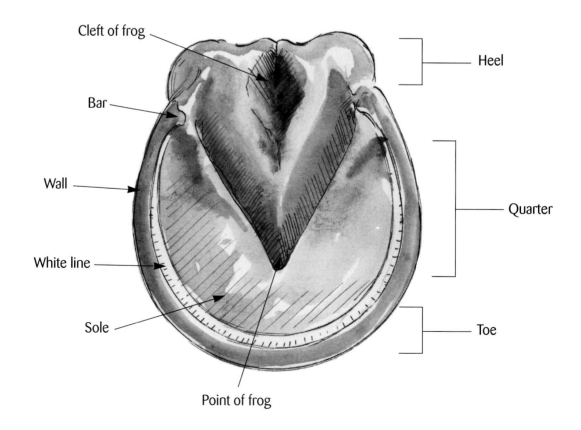

Cleft of frog

Heel

Bar

Wall

Quarter

White line

Sole

Toe

Point of frog

Glossary

Aids. Your signals; how you communicate with the horse.

Bars. Inside the horse's mouth, the gums between the incisors and the molars.

Bosal. A noseband of plaited rawhide, used as the controlling device in the hackamore.

Box. To hold or contain a cow in a certain area. Also, the roper's box.

Bridle. To maintain contact with the reins so the horse moves "in a frame" and "on the bit."

Bridle path. A clipped section of the mane, starting behind the ears.

Brindle dun. A dun body color with darker streaks.

Broke. Trained and reliable.

Bull pen. A training corral, also called a "round" pen.

Bump. To pull and release the reins for a brief contact with the horse's mouth.

Burner. A rawhide section on a rope, covering the eye of the hondo to protect the rope from wear.

Catch rope. A rope for catching cattle.

Chrome. Flashy white markings.

Chouse. To chase cattle, also to exhaust them.

Chute. In cattle events, a fenced lane that contains a single cow behind a gate.

Closed reins. Two reins connected to each other by a long, flexible quirt, the romal.

Coggins certificate. A veterinarian's document that certifies the horse free of the disease, equine infectious anemia.

Collect. To coordinate the horse's moving forward with impulsion while shortening the frame for slow motion.

Cone. A red vinyl traffic cone, used as a marker.

Consignor. The person who consigns a horse for sale or puts it up for auction.

Crupper. A strap that secures the saddle on a mule, running from the back of the saddle and under the mule's tail. Used only in trail riding.

Dally. To wind the rope end around the saddle horn.

Diagonal. At the trot, the movement of the horse's right and left shoulders. The rider posts with either diagonal. Also, a diagonal aid, such as inside rein and outside leg.

Double. To bend the horse sharply.

Drag. To hang back. Also, at the end of a column of riders, to "ride drag" or be a "drag rider."

Drop the shoulder. To shift weight on the forehand and lean too much to the inside during a turn.

Easyboot. A brand name for a vinyl boot that encloses the horse's hoof.

Engage. To shift weight to the hindquarters, to work off the hindquarters and stride forward with the hind legs.

Face. The horse's head. Also, to turn toward a cow.

Flank. In roping, to hold a calf by its flank and leg and place it on its side.

Flex. To bend the horse to the inside. Also, to give in the poll and yield to rein contact.

Flexion. A bend to the inside of a turn.

Flying change. A change of lead at the lope, without slowing to the trot.

Forehand. The horse's shoulders and front legs.

Four-beat. An incorrect lope, where the horse strikes the ground in a broken rhythm.

Futurity. A show class or event open to young horses that owners have nominated.

Go-round. A preliminary round. Some events have two or three go-rounds, and scores are averaged.

Ground tie. To stand in one place, with reins dropped on the ground.

Grulla. A dun body color that ranges from bluish gray to a brownish gray.

Gymkhana. A program of competitive games on horseback, usually timed events.

Hackamore. A bridle that uses a bosal.

Half hitch. A knot, also called a "hooey."

Header. In team roping, this rider ropes the steer's horns.

Headstalls. Another name for bridles.

Heeler. In team roping, this rider ropes the steer's heels.

High lope. A gallop.

Hobbles. Rope, cloth, or leather loops that fasten the forelegs together.

Hogtie. To tie three legs with a narrow rope.

Hondo. The eye on the end of a rope that forms the loop. Also called "honda."

Hooey. A half-hitch knot.

Impulsion. Forward energy.

In the hole. Third in line to enter the pen; after "on deck."

Inside. In a pen, the side of the horse toward the center.

Jerk. To pull or yank a rope or rein.

Junior. A horse four years old or younger; a rider 18 years or younger.

Kiss. A smacking noise made with the lips, to cue the horse to move forward.

Lateral. A sideways movement. Also, lateral aids, such as outside rein and outside leg.

Lead. During the lope, the horse's legs on one side stride forward first. The legs on one side hit the ground before and forward of the legs on the other side.

Legging up. Conditioning a horse's muscle tone by gradually increasing his work.

Long trot. An extended jog; a brisk trot.

Longe. To exercise a horse in a circle on a long lead rope (the longe line).

Loose rein. A slack rein.

Lope. To canter slowly.

Manty. A piece of canvas that encases the load tied on a pack animal.

Mark. To earn a score.

Marker. In reining and horsemanship, a location for the pattern.

Mecate. Braided horsehair reins; knotted to a bosal.

Near side. The horse's left side.

Neck rein. Movement of the rein against the horse's neck cues him to turn. Also called a "brace rein" or "bearing rein."

Neoprene. A synthetic rubber.

Non pro. An amateur, non-professional rider.

Off side. The horse's right side.

On deck. Next to go in the pen.

Outside. In a pen, the side of the horse toward the fence.

Overo. A Paint or Pinto coat pattern of spots that are irregular, scattered, or splashy. The horse usually has a large white facial marking as well.

P.A. The public address system in the arena or show pen.

Pattern. A course you follow in certain classes.

Pen. The show ring. Also to corral cattle, as in team penning.

Picket line. Rope tie rail.

Piggin string. A short, narrow rope used to hogtie a calf or steer.

Pitch. To loosen the reins abruptly and completely, or to toss a rope.

Pocket. A comfortable, secure place in the saddle. In timed events, the area where you collect the horse and start your turn around a barrel or pole.

Post. To rise from the saddle in rhythm with the horse's trot.

Prop. In timed events, a pole or barrel.

Quirt. A riding whip with a short handle and a rawhide lash.

Rail. The fenceline, as in a "rail" class.

Reata. A braided leather rope; coiled and fastened to a Western saddle.

Rigging. On a saddle, straps that connect the cinch and the saddle tree.

Romal. A leather quirt, attached to braided leather or rawhide reins, or "closed" reins.

Rope. A running noose. To catch a cow with the noose.

Rowel. A small wheel with points, attached to the shank of a spur.

Sclera. The area of the eye that encircles the cornea, the colored or pigmented portion.

Score. In roping, to break quickly to overtake the cow.

Scotch. In reining, to anticipate a stop by slowing the gallop.

Senior. A horse at least five years old. A rider at least 50 years old.

Serpentine. A winding pattern of loops or half-circles, in which the horse changes directions through the pattern.

Set. To fix, to establish. In cutting or team penning, a group of competitors that use the same group of cattle.

Settle. To group a bunch of cattle into a quiet, compact herd. Riders act as settlers to get the cattle used to horses moving around them.

Side pass. To move sideways, crossing one leg over another.

Slack. Loose rope or reins, or to loosen. In rodeo, the morning or afternoon performance.

Snatch. To jerk the reins sharply.

Steward. A show official who assists the judge in or out of the show pen.

String out. To move without engaging the hindquarters, so hind end looks "strung out" from the forehand.

Sull. To move slowly, to resist moving forward.

Tapadero. A leather hood fixed to the front of the stirrup.

Tiedown. A strap that connects to the noseband and the cinch or breastcollar; a control device to limit the height of the horse's head.

Tobiano. A Paint and Pinto coat pattern of spots that are regular and distinct.

Tovero. A Paint coat pattern that has markings of both the overo and the tobiano.

Track. A path. Also to follow.

Transition. Upward, the horse moves at a faster pace. Downward, the horse changes to a slower gait.

Two hand. To ride with one rein in each hand.

Two point. To rise from the saddle, so you contact the horse with only your thighs, not your seat.

Two-track. A lateral movement, where the horse's forefeet and hind feet move on separate tracks. Also called the half-pass.

Associations

Breed Associations

American Buckskin Registry
   Association
PO Box 3850
Redding, CA 96049-3850
916-223-1420

American Paint Horse
   Association
PO Box 961023
Fort Worth, TX 76161-0023
817-439-3400
Fax: 817-439-3484
Web: http://www.apha.com/
E-mail: http://www.apha.com/
   infobooth/Email/email.html

American Quarter Horse
   Association
PO Box 200
Amarillo, TX 79168
806-376-4888
Web: http://www.aqha.com

Appaloosa Horse Club
PO Box 8403
Moscow, ID 83843
208-882-5578
Web: http://www.appaloosa.com

International Buckskin Horse
   Association, Inc.
PO Box 268
Shelby, IN 46377
219-552-1013

National Quarter Pony
   Association, Inc.
PO Box 216
Baltimore, OH 43105
614-862-4023
Fax: 614-862-8674

Palomino Horse Breeders of
   America, Inc.
15253 E. Skelly Drive
Tulsa, OK 74116-2637
918-438-1234
Web: http://www.ansi.okstate.
   edu/phba/

Pinto Horse Association of
   America, Inc.
1900 Samuels Avenue
Fort Worth, TX 76102-1141
817-336-7842
Fax: 817-336-7416
Web: http://www.pinto.org/

Pony of the Americas Club, Inc.
5240 Elmwood Avenue
Indianapolis, IN 46203
317-788-0107

Spanish Barb Breeders
   Association
PO Box 598
Anthony, FL 32617
352-622-5878

Spanish Mustang Registry, Inc.
HCR 3, Box 7670
Wilcox, AZ 85643
520-384-2886

Show/Contest Associations

American Cutting Horse
   Association
PO Box 2568
Wimberley, TX 78676
512-847-6168

American Endurance Ride
   Conference
701 High Street, Suite 203
Auburn, CA 95603
916-823-2260
Fax: 916-823-7805
Web: http://www.aerc.com/
E-mail: aercride1@aol.com

American Horse Shows
   Association
220 East 42nd Street
New York, NY 10017-5876
212-972-2472

American Team Penning
   Championships
1776 Montano Road NW,
Building #3
Albuquerque, NM 87107
505-344-1776

International Halter-Pleasure
   Quarter Horse Association
11182 US Highway 69 N
Tyler, TX 75706

National Barrel Horse
   Association
PO Box 1988
Augusta, GA 30903
706-722-7223

National Cutting Horse
  Association
4704 Highway 377 South
Fort Worth, TX 76116
817-244-6188

National Reined Cow Horse
  Association
1318 Jepsen Avenue
Corcoran, CA 93212
209-992-9396

National Reining Horse
  Association
448 Main Street, Suite 204
Coshocton, OH 43143
614-623-0055
Web: http://www.nrha.com

National Snaffle Bit Association
One Indiana Square, Suite 2540
Indianapolis, IN 46204
317-632-NSBA

North American Trail Ride
  Conference
PO Box 2136
Ranchos de Taos, NM 87557
505-751-4198

U.S. Team Penning
  Association, Inc.
PO Box 161848
Fort Worth, TX 76161-1848
1-800-848-3882
817-439-0010
Web: http://www.tpaa.com

U.S. Team Roping
  Championships, Inc.
PO Box 7651
Albuquerque, NM 87194
505-899-1870

Youth Show and Contest Associations

Intercollegiate Horse Show
  Association
2109 Stillwell Beckett Road
Hamilton, OH 45013

National 4-H Council
7100 Connecticut Avenue
Chevy Chase, MD 20815-4999
301-961-2800
Fax: 301-961-2937
Web: http://ndsuext.nodak.edu/
  4h/natlcoun.htm

National Future Farmers of
  America Foundation
PO Box 45205
Madison, WI 53744-5205
608-829-3105
Web: http://www.agriculture.
  com/contents/FFA/index.html

National High School Rodeo
  Association, Inc.
11178 North Huron, Suite 7
Denver, CO 80234
303-452-0820

National Intercollegiate Rodeo
  Association
1815 Portland Avenue, #3
Walla Walla, WA 99362
509-529-4402

National Little Britches Rodeo
  Association
1045 West Rio Grande
Colorado Springs, CO 80906
719-389-0333

Ride and Tie Association
1865 Indian Valley Road
Novato, CA 94947
414-897-1829
Web: http://www.rideandtie.org

References

RULEBOOKS

American Endurance Ride Conference, Endurance Riders Handbook

American Buckskin Registry Association, Official Handbook

American Endurance Ride Conference, Rules and Regulations for Endurance Riding

American Horse Shows Association Rule Book

American Paint Horse Association, Official Rule Book

American Quarter Horse Association, Official Handbook

American Team Penning Championships

Appaloosa Horse Club, Official Handbook

International Buckskin Horse Association, Inc., Official Handbook

National Cutting Horse Association, Rule Book

National High School Rodeo Association, Rules, Constitution, and By-Laws

National Little Britches Rodeo Association, Revised Official Rule Book

National Reining Horse Association, Handbook

National Snaffle Bit Association, Official Handbook

North American Trail Ride Conference, Rule Book

Palomino Horse Breeders of America, Inc., Official Handbook

Pinto Horse Association of America, Inc., Official Handbook

U.S. Team Roping Championships, Inc.

BOOKS ON WESTERN RIDING

General

Foreman, Monte, and Patrick Wyse. *Monte Foreman's Horse-Training Science.* University of Oklahoma, 1983.

Forget, J.P. *The Complete Guide to Western Horsemanship.* Howel, 1995.

Jones, Suzanne Norton. *Art of Western Riding.* Wilshire, 1980.

Kirksmith, Tommie. *Ride Western Style.* Howell, 1991.

Kirksmith, Tommie. *Western Performance: A Guide for Young Riders.* Howell, 1993.

Mayhew, Bob. *Art of Western Riding.* Howell, 1990.

Strickland, Charlene. *Show Grooming: The Look of a Winner,* second edition. Breakthrough, 1995.

Strickland, Charlene. *Tack Buyers Guide.* Breakthrough, 1988.

Tellington-Jones, Linda, and Ursula Bruns. *Introduction to the Tellington-Jones Equine Awareness Method.* Breakthrough, 1988.

Specific Disciplines

Back, Joe. *Horses, Hitches, and Rocky Trails.* Johnson Publishing Company, 1959.

Camarillo, Leo. *Team Roping.* Western Horseman, 1982.

Camarillo, Sharon. *Barrel Racing.* Western Horseman, 1985.

Carpenter, Doug. *Western Pleasure: Training and Showing to Win.* EquiMedia, 1995.

Cooper, Roy. *Calf Roping.* Western Horseman, 1984.

Dunning, Al. *Reining.* Western Horseman, 1986.

Elser, Smoke, and Bill Brown. *Packin' In on Mules and Horses.* Mountain Press, 1980.

Freeman, Bill. *Cutting.* EquiMedia, 1994.

Harrell, Leon. *Cutting.* Western Horseman, 1989.

Harrison, Sally. *Cutting: A Guide for the Non-Pro Competitor.* Howell, 1992.

Livingston, Phil. *Team Penning.* Western Horseman, 1991.

Loomis, Bob. *Reining: The Art of Performance in Horses.* EquiMedia, 1990.

Loving, Nancy. *Go the Distance.* Trafalgar Square, 1998.

Paulo, Karen. *America's Long Distance Challenge.* Trafalgar Square, 1990 (out of print).

Shrake, Richard. *Western Horsemanship.* Western Horseman, 1987.

Index

Page references in *italics* indicate illustrations; **bold** indicates charts.

Other Storey Titles You Will Enjoy

Becoming an Effective Rider, by Cherry Hill. Teaches riders how to evaluate their own skills, plan a work session, set goals and achieve them, and protect themselves from injury. 192 pages. Paperback. ISBN 0-88266-688-6.

Competing in Western Shows and Events, by Charlene Strickland. Focuses on Western horse show basics, the rules and players, showing for intermediate riders, showing your work horse, timed events, and arena contests. 160 pages. Paperback. ISBN 1-58017-031-5.

From the Center of the Ring, by Cherry Hill. Covers all aspects of equestrian competition, both English and Western. 192 pages. Paperback. ISBN 0-88266-494-8.

Horse Handling & Grooming: A Step-by-Step Photographic Guide, by Cherry Hill. Includes feeding, haltering, tying, grooming, clipping, bathing, braiding, and blanketing. The wealth of practical advice offered is thorough enough for beginners, yet useful enough for experienced riders improving or expanding their skills. 144 pages. Paperback. ISBN 0-88266-956-7.

Horse Health Care: A Step-by-Step Photographic Guide, by Cherry Hill. Explains bandaging, giving shots, examining teeth, deworming, exercising, and preventive care. 160 pages. Paperback. ISBN 0-88266-955-9.

Horse Sense: A Complete Guide to Horse Selection & Care, by John J. Mettler, Jr., D.V.M. Provides the basics on selecting, housing, fencing, and feeding a horse including information on immunizations, dental care, and breeding. 160 pages. Paperback. ISBN 0-88266-545-6.

101 Arena Exercises, by Cherry Hill. This unique wire-bound ringside workout book can be hung up, or draped over the rail ring for easy reference. English and Western exercises are fully explained, from the basic skills such as the working walk and jog to the "two squares" and "flying change." 224 pages. Paperback. ISBN 0-88266-316-X.

Starting & Running Your Own Horse Business, by Mary Ashby McDonald. This essential guide shows readers how to run a successful business and how to make the most of their investments in horses, facilities, equipment, and time over short- and long-term periods. 160 pages. Paperback. ISBN 0-88266-960-5.

Teaching Safe Horsemanship: A Guide to English and Western Instruction, by Jan Dawson. Presents a step-by-step teaching program focusing on safety lessons, boarding, showing, and guest ranch activities. Explain protective release forms, insurance, and dealing with an accident or lawsuit. 160 pages. Hardcover. ISBN 0-88266-972-9.

These and other Storey books are available at your bookstore, farm store, garden center, or directly from Storey Books, Schoolhouse Road, Pownal, Vermont 05261, or by calling 1-800-441-5700. Visit our website at www.storey.com.